WORLD AT RISK

The Report of the Commission on the Prevention
of WMD Proliferation and Terrorism

WORLD AT RISK

The Report of the Commission on the Prevention of WMD Proliferation and Terrorism

Bob Graham, Chairman

Jim Talent, Vice-Chairman

**Graham Allison . Robin Cleveland
Steve Rademaker . Tim Roemer
Wendy Sherman . Henry Sokolski
Rich Verma**

VINTAGE BOOKS
A Division of Random House, Inc.
New York

First Vintage Books Edition: December 2008

THE AUTHORIZED EDITION of the *World at Risk: The Report of the Commission on the Prevention of WMD Proliferation and Terrorism* is published in the United States by Vintage Books, a division of Random House, Inc., New York, and in Canada by Random House of Canada Limited, Toronto.

ISBN: 978-0-307-47326-4

www.vintagebooks.com

www.preventwmd.gov

Printed in the United States of America

10 9 8 7 6 5 4 3 2 1

First Edition

Contents

ONE
Biological and Nuclear Risks 1

TWO
Findings and Recommendations 21

Appendices

December 2, 2008

The Honorable George W. Bush
President of the United States
Washington, D.C. 20500

Dear Mr. President:

In accordance with the Implementing Recommendations of the 9/11
Commission Act of 2007 (P.L. 110-53), we hereby submit the report of
the Commission on the Prevention of Weapons of Mass Destruction
Proliferation and Terrorism.

The mandate given to this Commission by Congress was far-
reaching. We were given a charter to assess, within 180 days, any and all
of the nation's activities, initiatives, and programs to prevent weapons of
mass destruction proliferation and terrorism. We were also asked to provide concrete recommendations—a road map, if you will—to address
these threats.

In response, we brought together a staff of more than two dozen
professionals and subject matter experts from across the national security, intelligence, and law enforcement communities. We interviewed
more than 250 government officials and nongovernmental experts. We
held eight major commission meetings and one public hearing.

Our research encompassed travel from the Sandia National Laboratory in New Mexico to London to Vienna. We traveled to Moscow to
assess U.S. nuclear cooperation initiatives with Russia. We were en
route to Pakistan, a country of particular interest to this Commission and
to the United States, only to hear that the bombing of the Marriott Hotel
in Islamabad had occurred. We had been hours from staying in that very
hotel.

Ultimately, we opted to center the Commission findings on several
areas where the risks to the United States are increasing: the crossroads

of terrorism and proliferation in the poorly governed parts of Pakistan, the prevention of biological and nuclear terrorism, and the potential erosion of international nuclear security, treaties, and norms as we enter a nuclear energy renaissance.

The intent of this report is neither to frighten nor to reassure the American people about the current state of terrorism and weapons of mass destruction. It is to underscore that the U.S. government has yet to fully adapt to these circumstances, and to convey the sobering reality that the risks are growing faster than our multilayered defenses. Our margin of safety is shrinking, not growing.

We thank you for the honor of allowing us to serve our country in this task. Our Commission and staff stand ready to help you in any way possible to explore and weigh the findings and recommendations contained in this report.

Respectfully submitted,

Senator Bob Graham
Chairman

Senator Jim Talent
Vice-Chairman

Dr. Graham T. Allison

Ms. Robin Cleveland

Mr. Stephen G. Rademaker

The Honorable Timothy J. Roemer

Ambassador Wendy R. Sherman

Mr. Henry D. Sokolski

Mr. Richard Verma

December 2, 2008

The Honorable Nancy Pelosi
United States House of Representatives
235 Cannon House Office Building
Washington, D.C. 20515

The Honorable John A. Boehner
United States House of Representatives
1011 Longworth House Office Building
Washington, D.C. 20515

The Honorable Harry Reid
United States Senate
528 Hart Senate Office Building
Washington, D.C. 20510

The Honorable Mitch McConnell
United States Senate
361-A Russell Senate Office Building
Washington, D.C. 20510

Dear Speaker Pelosi, Majority Leader Reid, Minority Leader Boehner, and Minority Leader McConnell:

In accordance with the Implementing Recommendations of the 9/11 Commission Act of 2007 (P.L. 110-53), we hereby submit the report of the Commission on the Prevention of Weapons of Mass Destruction Proliferation and Terrorism.

The mandate given to this Commission by Congress was far-reaching. We were given a charter to assess, within 180 days, any and all of the nation's activities, initiatives, and programs to prevent weapons of mass destruction proliferation and terrorism. We were also asked to provide concrete recommendations—a road map, if you will—to address these threats.

In response, we brought together a staff of more than two dozen professionals and subject matter experts from across the national security, intelligence, and law enforcement communities. We interviewed more than 250 government officials and nongovernmental experts. We held eight major commission meetings and one public hearing.

Our research encompassed travel from the Sandia National Laboratory in New Mexico to London to Vienna. We traveled to Moscow to assess U.S. nuclear cooperation initiatives with Russia. We were en route to Pakistan, a country of particular interest to this Commission and to the United States, only to hear that the bombing of the Marriott Hotel in Islamabad had occurred. We had been hours from staying in that very hotel.

Ultimately, we opted to center the Commission findings on several areas where the risks to the United States are increasing: the crossroads of terrorism and proliferation in the poorly governed parts of Pakistan, the prevention of biological and nuclear terrorism, and the potential erosion of international nuclear security, treaties, and norms as we enter a nuclear energy renaissance.

The intent of this report is neither to frighten nor to reassure the American people about the current state of terrorism and weapons of mass destruction. It is to underscore that the U.S. government has yet to fully adapt to these circumstances, and to convey the sobering reality that the risks are growing faster than our multilayered defenses. Our margin of safety is shrinking, not growing.

We thank you for the honor of allowing us to serve our country in this task. Our Commission and staff stand ready to help you in any way possible to explore and weigh the findings and recommendations contained in this report.

Respectfully submitted,

Senator Bob Graham
Chairman

Senator Jim Talent
Vice-Chairman

Dr. Graham T. Allison

Ms. Robin Cleveland

Mr. Stephen G. Rademaker

The Honorable Timothy J. Roemer

Ambassador Wendy R. Sherman

Mr. Henry D. Sokolski

Mr. Richard Verma

Preface

During the course of our fieldwork for this report, the members of the Commission had a near miss—and it served as a reminder of the urgency of our mission and message.

Asked by Congress to recommend ways of preventing weapons of mass destruction proliferation and terrorism, we were on our way to a place where these two concerns intersect—Pakistan. On September 20, 2008, we were in Kuwait City awaiting our connecting flight to Islamabad, where we would be staying at the Marriott Hotel. Suddenly our cell phones began buzzing with breaking news: the Islamabad Marriott had just been devastated by a bomb.

Minutes later, every television set in the airport was showing live footage of our destination. The Marriott was ablaze, a line of fire running its length. The hotel front was a mass of twisted iron and broken concrete. What once had been the lobby was now a huge black crater. More than fifty people lost their lives that day at the Islamabad Marriott, a gathering place for prominent visitors and influential locals. Within hours, the attack came to be known as Pakistan's 9/11—a frightening reminder that we live in an age of global terrorism.

The world is also imperiled by a new era of proliferation of weapons of mass destruction. Our Commission was charged with recommending ways of halting and reversing this proliferation. We focused on two categories of WMD—nuclear and biological weapons—because they pose the greatest peril.

The proliferation of these weapons increases the risk that they may be used in a terrorist attack in two ways. First, it increases the number of states that will be in a position either to use the weapons themselves or to transfer materials and know-how to those who might use WMD against us. The more proliferation that occurs, the greater the risk of additional proliferation, as nations that have to this point declined to acquire nuclear weapons will believe it necessary to counter their neighbors who have developed those capabilities. Second, it increases the prospect that these weapons will be poorly secured and thus may be stolen by terrorists or by others who intend to sell them to those who would do us harm.

Terrorists are determined to attack us again—with weapons of mass destruction if they can. Osama bin Laden has said that obtaining these weapons is a "religious duty" and is reported to have sought to perpetrate another "Hiroshima."

Our Commission is a legacy of the Joint Inquiry into Intelligence Community Activities Before and After the Terrorist Attacks of September 11, 2001, and the National Commission on Terrorist Attacks Upon the United States (the 9/11 Commission). The reports produced by these commissions explained to the American people how and why the U.S. government failed to discover that terrorists, operating from Afghanistan, were infiltrating the United States in order to use a most unconventional resource—commercial airplanes—as weapons that would kill thousands of people. We have a far different mandate: to examine the threats posed to the United States by weapons of mass destruction proliferation and terrorism in a world that has been changed forever by the forces of globalization.

The United States still wields enormous power of the traditional kind, but traditional power is less effective than it used to be. In today's world, individuals anywhere on the planet connect instantly with one another and with information. Money is moved, transactions are made, information is shared, instructions are issued, and attacks are unleashed with a keystroke. Weapons of tremendous destructive capability can be developed or acquired by those without access to an industrial base or even an economic base of any kind, and those weapons can be used to kill thousands of people and disrupt vital financial, communications, and transportation systems, which are easy to attack and hard to defend. All these factors have made nation-states less powerful and more vulnerable relative to the terrorists, who have no national base to defend and who therefore cannot be deterred through traditional means.

One of the purposes of this report is to set forth honestly and directly, for the consideration of the American people, the threat our country faces if terrorists acquire weapons of mass destruction. We also present recommendations of actions that the United States can undertake—unilaterally and in concert with the international community—to make our homeland and the world safer.

Though our recommendations are primarily addressed to the next President and the next Congress, we also envision an important role for citizens. We want to inform our fellow citizens, and thereby empower them to act. We call for a new emphasis on open and honest engagement between government and citizens in safeguarding our homeland and in becoming knowledgeable about and developing coordinated public responses to potential terrorist attacks.

In every terrorist strike anywhere in the world, to every innocent life lost must be added thousands more who were just hours away from having been at that ground zero, from having become innocent victims—a point powerfully underscored by the Commission's near miss on September 20, 2008. In those moments of danger, we are all, first and foremost, citizens of a world at risk, with the common cause of protecting the innocent and preserving our way of life.

It is our hope to break the all-too-familiar cycle in which disaster strikes and a commission is formed to report to us about what our government should have known and done to keep us safe. This time we do know. We know the threat we face. We know that our margin of safety is shrinking, not growing. And we know what we must do to counter the risk. There is no excuse now for allowing domestic partisanship or international rivalries to prevent or delay the actions that must be taken. We need unity at all levels—nationally, locally, and among people all across the globe. There is still time to defend ourselves, if we act with the urgency called for by the nature of the threat that confronts us. Sounding that call for urgent action is the purpose of this report.

Executive Summary

The Commission believes that unless the world community acts decisively and with great urgency, it is more likely than not that a weapon of mass destruction will be used in a terrorist attack somewhere in the world by the end of 2013.

The Commission further believes that terrorists are more likely to be able to obtain and use a biological weapon than a nuclear weapon. The Commission believes that the U.S. government needs to move more aggressively to limit the proliferation of biological weapons and reduce the prospect of a bioterror attack.

Further compounding the nuclear threat is the proliferation of nuclear weapons capabilities to new states and the decision by several existing nuclear states to build up their arsenals. Such proliferation is a concern in its own right because it may increase the prospect of military crises that could lead to war and catastrophic use of these weapons. As former Senator Sam Nunn testified to our Commission: "The risk of a nuclear weapon being used today is growing, not receding."

This Commission was chartered by Congress to assess our nation's progress in preventing weapons of mass destruction proliferation and terrorism—and to provide the next President and Congress with concrete, actionable recommendations that can serve as their road map to a safer homeland and world.

No mission could be timelier. The simple reality is that the risks that confront us today are evolving faster than our multilayered responses. Many thousands of dedicated people across all agencies of our government are working hard to protect this country, and their efforts have had a positive impact. But the terrorists have been active, too—and in our judgment America's margin of safety is shrinking, not growing.

The Commission reached that sobering conclusion following six months of deliberations, site visits, and interviews with more than 250 government officials and nongovernmental experts in the United States and abroad.

While the mandate of the Commission was to examine the full sweep of the challenges posed by the nexus of terrorist activity and the proliferation of all forms of WMD—chemical, biological, radiological, and nuclear—we concluded early in our deliberations that this report should focus solely on the two types of WMD categories that have the greatest potential to kill in the most massive numbers: biological and nuclear weapons.

Since the end of the Cold War, the United States has spent billions of dollars securing nuclear weapons, materials, and technology in Russia and the former states of the Soviet Union—to good effect—and has introduced some new counterproliferation measures. But during that period, the world has also witnessed a new era of proliferation: North Korea tested a nuclear weapon; Iran has been rapidly developing capabilities that will enable it to build nuclear weapons; Dr. A. Q. Khan, of Pakistan, led a nuclear proliferation network that was a one-stop shop for aspiring nuclear weapons countries; and nuclear arms rivalries have intensified in the Middle East and Asia. If not constrained, this proliferation could prompt nuclear crises and even nuclear use at the very time that the United States and Russia are trying to reduce their nuclear weapons deployments and stockpiles.

Meanwhile, biotechnology has spread globally. At the same time that it has benefited humanity by enabling advances in medicine and in agriculture, it has also increased the availability of pathogens and technologies that can be used for sinister purposes. Many biological pathogens and nuclear materials around the globe are poorly secured—and thus vulnerable to theft by those who would put these materials to harmful use, or would sell them on the black market to potential terrorists.

According to an April 2006 National Intelligence Estimate on Trends in Global Terrorism, "Activists identifying themselves as jihadists, although a small percentage of Muslims, are increasing both in number and geographic dispersion. . . . If this trend continues, threats to U.S. interests at home and abroad will become more diverse, leading to increasing attacks worldwide." Since 9/11 there has been an increase in the number of groups that have associated or aligned themselves with al Qaeda—the preeminent terrorist threat to the United States and the perpetrators of 9/11—including al Qaeda in Iraq, the Libyan Islamic Fighting Group, and the Algerian al Qaeda in the Islamic Maghreb, formerly the Salafist Group for Preaching and Combat (GSPC). This increase in terrorist networks is a threat to the entire world.

Though U.S. policy and strategy have made progress, they have not kept pace with the growing risks. In the area of counterterrorism, our government has innovated and implemented new initiatives since 9/11, but its focus has been mainly limited to defense, intelligence, and homeland security programs and operations. The next administration needs to go much further, using the tools of "soft power" to communicate effectively about American intentions and to build grassroots social and economic institutions that will discourage radicalism and undercut the terrorists in danger spots around the world—especially in Pakistan.

Biological Proliferation and Terrorism

Since terrorists attacked the United States on September 11, 2001, the U.S. government has addressed the risk of biological proliferation and terrorism with policies rooted in a far different mind-set than the one that guides its policies toward nuclear weapons. While U.S. strategies to combat nuclear terrorism focus on securing the world's stocks of fissile materials before terrorists can steal or buy enough on the black market to build a nuclear bomb, the government's approach to bioterrorism has placed too little emphasis on prevention. The Commission believes that the United States must place a greater emphasis on the prevention side of the equation.

To date, the U.S. government has invested the largest portion of its nonproliferation efforts and diplomatic capital in preventing nuclear terrorism. Only by elevating the priority of preventing bioterrorism will it be possible to substantially improve U.S. and global biosecurity.

The nuclear age began with a mushroom cloud—and, from that moment on, all those who worked in the nuclear industry in any capacity, military or civilian, understood they must work and live under a clear and undeniable security mandate. But the life sciences community has never experienced a comparable iconic event. As a result, security awareness has grown slowly, lagging behind the emergence of biological risks and threats. It is essential that the members of the life sciences community—in universities, medical and veterinary schools, nongovernmental research institutes, trade associations, and biotechnology and pharmaceutical companies—foster a bottom-up effort to sensitize researchers to biosecurity issues and concerns.

RECOMMENDATION 1: The United States should undertake a series of mutually reinforcing domestic measures to prevent bioterrorism: (1) conduct a comprehensive review of the domestic program to secure dangerous pathogens, (2) develop a national strategy for advancing bioforensic capabilities, (3) tighten government oversight of high-containment laboratories, (4) promote a culture of security awareness in the life sciences community, and (5) enhance the nation's capabilities for rapid response to prevent biological attacks from inflicting mass casualties.

∘ ∘ ∘

The cornerstone of international efforts to prevent biological weapons proliferation and terrorism is the 1972 Biological Weapons Convention (BWC). This treaty bans the development, production, and acquisition of biological and toxin weapons and the delivery systems specifically designed for their dispersal. But because biological activities, equipment, and technology can be used for good as well as harm, BW-related activities are exceedingly difficult to detect, rendering traditional verification measures ineffective. In addition, the globalization of the life sciences and technology has created new risks of misuse by states and terrorists.

The BWC has been undercut by serious violations, which went undetected for years, and by its failure to gain universal membership. Moreover, the treaty is not supported at the international level by an overarching strategy for preventing biological weapons proliferation and terrorism.

Meanwhile, U.S. biological cooperative threat reduction (CTR) programs in the former Soviet Union (FSU) have made good progress in improving pathogen security and in redirecting former bioweapons scientists to peaceful activities. In recent years, however, the Russian government has viewed such programs with disinterest and even suspicion and has argued that its growing economic strength obviates the need for continued foreign assistance. Bureaucratic and political obstacles in Russia have forced the United States to reluctantly cut back its biological CTR activities there. The security of pathogen collections in Russia has been improved, but the large cadre of former bioweapons scientists remains a global proliferation concern.

Although biological CTR programs have stalled in Russia, the U.S. government has expanded them elsewhere. The program now includes developing countries in the Middle East, South Asia, and Southeast Asia that face significant risks from transnational terrorist groups, have poorly secured biological laboratories and culture collections, and experience frequent outbreaks of emerging infectious diseases. To prevent terrorists from stealing dangerous pathogens or recruiting indigenous biological experts, the United States has helped these countries upgrade laboratory security, has provided biosecurity training, and has engaged hundreds of life scientists in peaceful research projects. These efforts are ongoing, and it remains to be seen if they will be successful. Other parts of the developing world, including Africa and South America, face serious biosecurity challenges and could benefit from similar cooperative threat reduction programs.

RECOMMENDATION 2: The United States should undertake a series of mutually reinforcing measures at the international level to prevent biological weapons proliferation and terrorism: (1) press for an international conference of countries with major biotechnology industries to promote biosecurity, (2) conduct a global assessment of biosecurity risks, (3) strengthen global disease surveillance networks, and (4) propose a new action plan for achieving universal adherence to and effective national implementation of the Biological Weapons Convention, for adoption at the next review conference in 2011.

Nuclear Proliferation and Terrorism

The number of states that are armed with nuclear weapons or are seeking to develop them is increasing. Terrorist organizations are intent on acquiring nuclear weapons or the material and expertise needed to build them. Trafficking in nuclear materials and technology is a serious, relentless, and multidimensional problem.

Yet nuclear terrorism is still a preventable catastrophe. The world must move with new urgency to halt the proliferation of nuclear weapons nations—and the United States must increase its global leadership efforts to stop the proliferation of nuclear weapons and safeguard nuclear material before it falls into the hands of terrorists. The new administration must move to revitalize the Nuclear Nonproliferation Treaty (NPT).

The nonproliferation regime embodied in the NPT has been eroded and the International Atomic Energy Agency's financial resources fall far short of its existing and expanding mandate. The amount of safeguarded nuclear bomb-making material has grown by a factor of 6 to 10 over the past 20 years, while the agency's safeguards budget has not kept pace and the number of IAEA inspections per facility has actually declined.

RECOMMENDATION 3: The United States should work internationally toward strengthening the nonproliferation regime, reaffirming the vision of a world free of nuclear weapons by (1) imposing a range of penalties for NPT violations and withdrawal from the NPT that shift the burden of proof to the state under review for noncompliance; (2) ensuring access to nuclear fuel, at market prices to the extent possible, for non-nuclear states that agree not to develop sensitive fuel cycle capabilities and are in full compliance with international obligations; (3) strengthening the International Atomic Energy Agency, to include identifying the limitations to its safeguarding capabilities, and providing the agency with the resources and authorities needed to meet its current and expanding mandate; (4) promoting the further development and effective implementation of counterproliferation initiatives such as the Proliferation Security Initiative and the Global Initiative to Combat Nuclear Terrorism; (5) orchestrating consensus that there will be no new states, including Iran and North Korea, possessing uranium enrichment or plutonium-reprocessing capability; (6) working in concert with others to do everything possible to promote and maintain a moratorium on nuclear testing; (7) working toward a global agreement on the definition of "appropriate" and "effective" nuclear security and accounting systems as legally obligated under United

Nations Security Council Resolution 1540; and (8) discouraging, to the extent possible, the use of financial incentives in the promotion of civil nuclear power.

○ ○ ○

The United States and Russia together possess about 95 percent of the world's nuclear material. This fact has led the United States to work closely with Russia to make sure that all of this material is safe from theft and that Russia's former WMD scientists find employment outside of the nuclear military complex. The United States has spent billions of dollars securing nuclear weapons, materials, and technology in Russia and the former states of the Soviet Union. Now Russia is a full partner and the two countries must work together to help other states improve their nuclear security and safety.

Cooperative nuclear security programs, part of the overall effort by the United States to address proliferation and WMD terrorist threats, can be better utilized. To date, such cooperative programs have focused on Russia. Although there is more to do there, the next President should build on work already under way to involve all nations in the fight against proliferation and WMD terrorism.

RECOMMENDATION 4: The new President should undertake a comprehensive review of cooperative nuclear security programs, and should develop a global strategy that accounts for the worldwide expansion of the threat and the restructuring of our relationship with Russia from that of donor and recipient to a cooperative partnership.

○ ○ ○

The Commission focused with special urgency on the pressing nuclear proliferation designs of two nations, one with ties to terrorists and both with records of weapons proliferation: Iran and North Korea. The Commission believes strongly that the United States, together with other nations, must develop the right combination of incentives and disincentives to address these problem cases. The Commission views the nation's fundamental objectives as clear and compelling: Iran must cease all of its efforts to develop nuclear weapons; North Korea must dismantle its nuclear program. Smart diplomacy requires that any approach be coupled with the credible threat of direct action to ensure we meet these objectives.

Iran continues to defy its NPT obligations, UN Security Council resolutions, and the international community in an apparent effort to acquire a nuclear weapons capability. It has 3,850 centrifuges spinning and more than 1,000 pounds of enriched uranium—three-quarters of what would be needed, after further enrichment, to build its first bomb.

Meanwhile, there has been at least some progress in the international efforts to convince North Korea to roll back its nuclear program. The February 2007 Six-Party Agreement on a concrete denuclearization plan was a first step toward the realization of a non-nuclear Korean peninsula. After months of glacial diplomatic movement, progress has recently been made on framing the verification issues. However, it remains uncertain whether Pyongyang will ultimately carry out its commitment to eliminate its nuclear weapons and associated enrichment and reprocessing capabilities. Experts say that North Korea now has about 10 bombs' worth of plutonium and it has conducted a nuclear test.

The Commission decided that because of the dynamic international environment, it would not address the precise tactics that should be employed by the next administration to achieve the strategic objective of stopping the nuclear weapons programs of these two countries. Developing those tactical initiatives will clearly be one of its urgent priorities.

But on the central finding, the Commission was unanimous in concluding that the nuclear aspirations of Iran and North Korea pose immediate and urgent threats to the Nuclear Nonproliferation Treaty. Successful nuclear programs in both countries could trigger a cascade of proliferation and lead to the unraveling of the NPT.

RECOMMENDATION 5: As a top priority, the next administration must stop the Iranian and North Korean nuclear weapons programs. In the case of Iran, this requires the permanent cessation of all of Iran's nuclear weapons–related efforts. In the case of North Korea, this requires the complete abandonment and dismantlement of all nuclear weapons and existing nuclear programs. If, as appears likely, the next administration seeks to stop these programs through direct diplomatic engagement with the Iranian and North Korean governments, it must do so from a position of strength, emphasizing both the benefits to them of abandoning their nuclear weapons programs and the enormous costs of failing to do so. Such engagement must be backed by the credible threat of direct action in the event that diplomacy fails.

Pakistan: The Intersection of Nuclear Weapons and Terrorism

Were one to map terrorism and weapons of mass destruction today, all roads would intersect in Pakistan. It has nuclear weapons and a history of unstable governments, and parts of its territory are currently a safe haven for al Qaeda and other terrorists. Moreover, given Pakistan's tense relationship with India, its buildup of nuclear weapons is exacerbating the prospect of a dangerous nuclear arms race in South Asia that could lead to a nuclear conflict.

Pakistan is an ally, but there is a grave danger it could also be an unwitting source of a terrorist attack on the United States—possibly with weapons of mass destruction.

Our Commission has singled out Pakistan for special attention in this report, as we believe it poses a serious challenge to America's short-term and medium-term national security interests. Indeed, many government officials and outside experts believe that the next terrorist attack against the United States is likely to originate from within the Federally Administered Tribal Areas (FATA) in Pakistan. The Commission agrees. In terms of the nexus of proliferation and terrorism, Pakistan must top the list of priorities for the next President and Congress.

RECOMMENDATION 6: The next President and Congress should implement a comprehensive policy toward Pakistan that works with Pakistan and other countries to (1) eliminate terrorist safe havens through military, economic, and diplomatic means; (2) secure nuclear and biological materials in Pakistan; (3) counter and defeat extremist ideology; and (4) constrain a nascent nuclear arms race in Asia.

Russia and the United States

Of all America's interests involving Russia, none is more vital than reducing the risk of the accidental or intentional use of nuclear and biological weapons against our nation and its allies from a source in Russia.

As great powers with divergent interests, the United States and Russia inevitably will have disagreements. But both governments have a responsibility to prevent these disagreements from interfering with their critical mutual interests—preventing the proliferation and use of nuclear and biological weapons and keeping WMD out of the hands of terrorists. The two countries also have a common interest in pursuing further strategic nuclear reductions.

RECOMMENDATION 7: The next U.S. administration should work with the Russian government on initiatives to jointly reduce the danger of the use of nuclear and biological weapons, including by (1) extending some of the essential verification and monitoring provisions of the Strategic Arms Reduction Treaty that are scheduled to expire in 2009; (2) advancing cooperation programs such as the Global Initiative to Combat Nuclear Terrorism, United Nations Security Council Resolution 1540, and the Proliferation Security Initiative; (3) sustaining security upgrades at sensitive sites in Russia and elsewhere, while finding common ground on further reductions in stockpiles of excess highly enriched uranium; (4) jointly encouraging China, Pakistan, and India to announce a moratorium on the further production of nuclear fissile materials for nuclear weapons and to reduce existing nuclear military deployments and stockpiles; and (5) offering assistance to other nations, such as Pakistan and India, in achieving nuclear confidence-building measures similar to those that the United States and the USSR followed for most of the Cold War.

Government Organization and Culture

Although in 2004 the two major party presidential candidates agreed that the biggest threat to the United States was WMD terrorism, today there is still no single high-level individual or office responsible for directing U.S. policy to prevent WMD proliferation and terrorism. The Commission is also concerned that in numerous cases in which policy trade-offs were required, nonproliferation was viewed as a secondary security issue. It is critical to have a senior official with direct access to the President to direct and promote nonproliferation interests.

This shortcoming is compounded by the fact that the President's policymaking on WMD proliferation and terrorism is overseen by two parallel staffs—one team working for the National Security Council (NSC) and the other working for the Homeland Security Council (HSC). Senior officials must deal with time-consuming meetings and overlapping responsibilities. The greatest threat to our nation is managed across many offices, rather than by one high-level office dedicated to this single issue.

RECOMMENDATION 8: The President should create a more efficient and effective policy coordination structure by designating a White House principal advisor for WMD proliferation and terrorism and restructuring the National Security Council and Homeland Security Council.

○ ○ ○

While Congress has been forceful in demanding reform of the executive branch, it has been slow to heed calls from others to reform itself. Prior commissions, including the 9/11 Commission, have called for reforming congressional committee jurisdiction and oversight. Congress has made some initial progress, yet much more needs to be done.

Consistent with findings of the 9/11 Commission and other previous commissions, congressional oversight remains dysfunctional. The existing committee structure does not allow for effective oversight of crosscutting national security threats, such as WMD proliferation and terrorism.

RECOMMENDATION 9: Congress should reform its oversight both structurally and substantively to better address intelligence, homeland security, and crosscutting 21st-century national security missions such as the prevention of weapons of mass destruction proliferation and terrorism.

○ ○ ○

In response to the Intelligence Reform and Terrorism Prevention Act of 2004, the intelligence community is implementing the most sweeping organizational changes since 1947. The community has achieved significant progress in a relatively short period of time and is currently engaged in a number of promising internal initiatives. Every effort should be made to accelerate those reforms. However, under the circumstances, the Commission believes that Congress and the administration should oversee and observe the results of current efforts before initiating further organizational change, though such changes might well be necessary in the future. One area should be the focus of special effort: the intelligence community still has insufficient personnel who have the critical skills needed to improve our nation's effort to stop proliferators and terrorists.

RECOMMENDATION 10: Accelerate integration of effort among the counterproliferation, counterterrorism, and law enforcement communities to address WMD proliferation and terrorism issues; strengthen expertise in the nuclear and biological fields; prioritize pre-service and in-service training and retention of people with critical scientific, language, and foreign area skills; and ensure that the threat posed by biological weapons remains among the highest national intelligence priorities for collection and analysis.

○ ○ ○

Despite recent initiatives, the national security agencies, including the national laboratories, still lack the flexibility and workforce culture they need to attract, train, and retain individuals with the skills necessary to effectively respond to globalized, networked threats.

RECOMMENDATION 11: The United States must build a national security workforce for the 21st century.

○ ○ ○

While the United States has had success in eliminating a number of terrorist leaders and foiling planned attacks, our government has invested less effort, let alone enjoyed success, at preventing the global recruitment and ideological commitment of extremists who might seek to use nuclear or biological weapons against America or its allies. These efforts demand an approach far different from that used to capture or kill terrorists and facilitators. They require the tools of soft power, which include the ability to communicate persuasively about American intentions and to assist in promoting social and economic progress within those countries where the terrorists have a recruiting presence. Government agencies must think creatively to develop and coordinate efforts—ranging from strategic communications to targeted development assistance—to engage those who might otherwise be drawn to terrorist causes.

RECOMMENDATION 12: U.S. counterterrorism strategy must more effectively counter the ideology behind WMD terrorism. The United States should develop a more coherent and sustained strategy and capabilities for global ideological engagement to prevent future recruits, supporters, and facilitators.

The Role of the Citizen

A well informed and mobilized citizenry has long been one of our nation's greatest resources. The next administration therefore should, within six months, work with state and local governments to develop a checklist of actions that need to be taken to improve efforts at all levels of government to prevent WMD proliferation and terrorism. Citizens should hold their governments accountable for completing this checklist.

Insufficient effort has been made to engage the public in the prevention of WMD terrorism, even though public tips have provided clues necessary to disrupt terrorist plots against the homeland. We need to give our citizens guidance on what to expect from their government at all levels and on how to be engaged in the prevention of WMD terrorism.

RECOMMENDATION 13: The next administration must work to openly and honestly engage the American citizen, encouraging a participatory approach to meeting the challenges of the new century.

∘ ∘ ∘

We decided at the beginning of our deliberations that we would be direct and honest with the American people about the challenges we confront. That is why we have not hesitated to state our conclusion that America's margin of safety against a WMD attack is shrinking. But we also want to assure the people that there is ample and solid ground for hope about the future. Our leaders—whatever their differences over domestic issues—are united in their desire to safeguard our country. The vast majority of the world's peoples stand with us in wanting to prevent the use of weapons of mass destruction and to defeat terrorists. Our nation has immense reservoirs of strength that we have only begun to use, and our enemies have weaknesses that we are learning how to exploit. There is much more that we can do to protect ourselves. In this report we lay out the steps that need to be taken, with confidence that they *will* be taken, and that as a result the United States, leading the international community, will have enhanced the safety of our world at risk.

ONE

Biological and Nuclear Risks

The greatest danger of another catastrophic attack in the United States will materialize if the world's most dangerous terrorists acquire the world's most dangerous weapons.

—*The 9/11 Commission Report*

Biological Risks

They were agents on a mission and they came not at night, which might have looked suspicious, but in broad daylight. Hiding in plain sight on a city street in Atlanta, they walked the perimeter of one of America's five biological laboratories where scientists worked on the world's most deadly pathogens. They had come to this lab at Georgia State University in 2008 as part of their assignment to quietly case facilities designated as Biosafety Level 4 (BSL-4) labs, the highest level of biological containment, required for work with the most dangerous viruses. They were looking for even the slightest security vulnerability—anything that might give an edge to terrorists seeking to steal small quantities of Ebola virus or other lethal disease agents for which there are no treatments, no known cures.

These individuals discovered that in a number of places, the lab was unprotected by barriers and that outsiders could walk right up to the building housing these deadly pathogens. Around back, they watched and took notes as a pedestrian simply strolled into the building through an unguarded loading dock.

On another day, the same people went to San Antonio to check out another BSL-4 lab, the Southwest Foundation for Biomedical Research. They discovered that the security camera covered only a portion of the perimeter, and that the only barrier to vehicles was an arm gate that would swing across the roadway. The guards assigned to protect this facility were unarmed. Once again, these individuals walked the perimeter. This time they spotted a window through which, standing outside, they could watch the scientists as they worked with top-security pathogens. Now they knew exactly where the world's most deadly pathogens were kept.

This was precisely the lethal trove that al Qaeda's terrorists had been seeking for years. But luckily, these operatives on this mission were not from al Qaeda—they were from the Government Accountability Office (GAO), the investigative arm of the U.S. Congress, and they visited five of America's labs that are designated BSL-4. For more than a decade, U.S. government inspection teams have traveled to facilities in the former Soviet Union and reported back on the poor security and lax practices used in storing biological pathogens. Now, this latest study by GAO has shown that when it comes to materials of bioterrorism, America's vulnerability may well begin at home.

The GAO report gave high marks to three of the five facilities investigated. The investigators measured how the labs fared in 15 security control categories, and these labs met the standards for, respectively, 13, 14, and all 15. Among the 15 security controls were having armed security guards visible at all public entrances to the lab, full camera coverage of all exterior entrances, and closed-circuit television and a command and control center so that any security breach could be instantly known throughout the facility.

But the two lowest-scoring BSL-4 labs passed in only 3 and 4 of the 15 categories—a score that is even more troubling because, as GAO noted, both still met the requirements of the Division of Select Agents and Toxins of the Centers for Disease Control and Prevention (CDC).

Despite these shortcomings, the United States is actually at the forefront of laboratory security in the world today and has by far the most stringent regulations to restrict access to dangerous pathogens. Most developing countries, in contrast, have largely ignored the problem of biosecurity because of competing demands for their limited budgets. Security gaps at laboratories that store and work with dangerous pathogens, both in the United States and around the world, are worrisome because of continued interest in biological weapons. Director of National Intelligence Michael McConnell said in a recent speech, "One of our greatest concerns continues to be that a terrorist group or some other dangerous group might acquire and employ biological agents . . . to create casualties greater than September 11."

Al Qaeda has long sought to obtain biological and chemical weapons. One of its leading experts in the quest for such weapons was Midhat Mursi al-Sayid Umar, an Egyptian also known as Abu Khabab al-Masri. According to media accounts, he was killed in July 2008 by an airstrike over Pakistan's northern tribal area.

On July 17, 2008, the Afghanistan National Police arrested Aafia

Siddiqui, a Pakistani woman believed to have ties to al Qaeda, who reportedly had been acting suspiciously outside the governor's compound in Ghazni province. Educated at the Massachusetts Institute of Technology and at Brandeis University, where she earned a Ph.D. in neuroscience, she had been wanted by the FBI since 2004—the first woman sought by the law enforcement agency in connection with al Qaeda. According to media accounts, when arrested she had in her possession a list of New York City landmarks, documents describing how to produce explosives, and details about chemical, biological, and radiological weapons. She was extradited to New York for trial on charges of attempted murder and assault of U.S. officers in Afghanistan.

The world is fortunate that al Qaeda to date is not known to have successfully stolen, bought, or developed agents of bioterror. But scenarios of just how such an incident might occur have been developed for planning purposes. The Homeland Security Council has created a chilling scenario of how terrorists could launch an anthrax attack in the United States—and the horrific chain of events that would follow:

> This scenario describes a single aerosol [anthrax] attack in one city delivered by a truck using a concealed improvised spraying device in a densely populated urban city with a significant commuter workforce. It does not, however, exclude the possibility of multiple attacks in disparate cities or time-phased attacks (i.e., "reload"). For federal planning purposes, it will be assumed that the Universal Adversary (UA) will attack five separate metropolitan areas in a sequential manner. Three cities will be attacked initially, followed by two additional cities 2 weeks later.
>
> It is possible that a Bio-Watch [atmospheric sensor] signal would be received and processed, but this is not likely to occur until the day after the release. The first cases of anthrax would begin to present to Emergency Rooms (ERs) approximately 36 hours post-release, with rapid progression of symptoms and fatalities in untreated (or inappropriately treated) patients.
>
> The situation in the hospitals will be complicated by the following facts: The release has occurred at the beginning of an unusually early influenza season and the prodromal [early]

symptoms of inhalation anthrax are relatively non-specific. Physician uncertainty will result in low thresholds for admission and administration of available countermeasures (e.g., antibiotics), producing severe strains on commercially available supplies of medications such as ciprofloxacin and doxycycline, and exacerbating the surge capacity problem.

Social order questions will arise. The public will want to know very quickly if it is safe to remain in the affected city and surrounding regions. Many persons will flee regardless of the public health guidance that is provided. Pressure may be placed directly on pharmacies to dispense medical countermeasures directly, and it will be necessary to provide public health guidance in more than a dozen languages.

The attack results in 328,848 exposures; 13,208 untreated fatalities; and 13,342 total casualties. Although property damage will be minimal, city services will be hampered by safety concerns.

000

In September 2001, an American public already reeling from the worst terrorist attack in U.S. history was stunned by news that envelopes containing anthrax had been delivered via the U.S. mail to targets in the news media. A week after September 11, letters containing 1–2 grams of dried anthrax bacterial spores were sent to three major television broadcast networks, the *New York Post,* and American Media International (AMI) in Florida, a publisher of supermarket tabloids. On October 5, the tainted letters claimed their first victim: Robert Stevens, a photo editor at AMI, died of inhalational anthrax. On October 9, two more letters bearing the same New Jersey postmark and containing a more refined preparation of dried anthrax spores were mailed to the Washington, D.C., offices of Senators Tom Daschle and Patrick Leahy.

During their journey, the anthrax letters passed through automated mail-sorting machines that forced the microscopic anthrax spores out through tiny pores in the envelopes, thereby infecting a number of postal workers. The tainted sorting machines also cross-contaminated other letters, which were delivered and sickened some of their recipients. By November 2001, 22 people in New York, New Jersey, Connecticut, Florida, and the District of Columbia had contracted anthrax, half of them through the skin (causing cutaneous anthrax) and the other half through the lungs (causing inhalational anthrax). Five of the 11 victims who contracted inhalational anthrax died.

Former NBC news anchor Tom Brokaw, who was one of the targets of the anthrax letters, testified about his experience at the Commission's public hearing in New York City. About a week after September 11, 2001, Brokaw said, two of his assistants handled a letter addressed to him that contained a granular powder. Several days after coming in contact with the powder, both women developed fever, malaise, and ugly black skin lesions. Their mysterious illness touched off several days of confusion and missteps. Three times Brokaw was told by various health officials, including experts at the U.S. Army's biodefense research center at Fort Detrick, in Maryland, that his assistants' skin lesions had been caused by the bite of a brown recluse spider. Finally, nearly three weeks after the initial exposures, officials from the U.S. Centers for Disease Control and Prevention (CDC) made the correct diagnosis of cutaneous anthrax. Prior to this diagnosis, Brokaw recalled, there was "kind of an unsettled feeling in the [NBC] building, but we're confining it because we don't want to cause undue panic. You know, we're operating based on what we've been told by very authoritative sources. Well, when we're told that it is in fact an anthrax attack, that [my assistants] have cutaneous anthrax, all hell broke loose at 30 Rock. There were no [response] systems in place."

In August 2008, the Department of Justice declared that it had identified the perpetrator of the 2001 anthrax attacks as Bruce E. Ivins, a government biodefense scientist who had worked for decades at the U.S. Army's biodefense research laboratory at Fort Detrick. Ivins had committed suicide shortly before he was to be indicted for the crime.

The anthrax mailings revealed serious gaps in U.S. preparedness for bioterrorism that have been only partly addressed over the past seven years. Since 2001, however, no further bioterrorist attacks have occurred. What is the risk of another incident? How worried should the public be? And in the future, how will the bioscience revolution and the globalization of the biotechnology industry change the nature of the biological weapons threat?

Biological and Nuclear Risks

What Are Biological Weapons?

Biological weapons are disease-causing microbes (chiefly bacteria and viruses) and toxins (poisonous substances produced by living creatures) that have been harnessed for the purpose of incapacitating or killing humans, livestock, or crops. Examples include the bacteria that cause anthrax and plague, the viruses that cause smallpox and Ebola hemorrhagic fever, and poisons of natural origin such as ricin and botulinum toxin.

Each of these agents has distinct characteristics that affect its suitability for use as a weapon. These are *infectivity* (the ability to infect a human host and cause disease), *virulence* (the severity of the resulting illness), *transmissibility* (the ability of the disease to spread from person to person), and *persistence* (the duration of a microbe's survival after its release into the environment).

The process of turning a natural pathogen into a WMD begins with acquiring a sample of a disease-causing microbe from a natural source (such as a person or sick animal) or stealing it from a laboratory or culture collection. But just as a bullet is a harmless lump of lead without a cartridge and a rifle to deliver it, so most pathogens and toxins are not effective weapons in their natural state and must be processed ("weaponized") and combined with a delivery system to make them capable of producing large numbers of casualties.

The anthrax bacterium is considered an ideal biological warfare agent because it is relatively easy to grow, highly lethal when inhaled, and able to transform itself into a hearty spore that can persist in soil or contaminate a target area for years. If an individual is treated with antibiotics shortly after inhaling anthrax spores, the infection can usually be cured. If treatment is delayed, however, the bacterial toxins will be released, and extraordinary medical intervention is then needed for the victim to have any chance of survival.

Despite the small quantity of dried anthrax spores used in the 2001 letter attacks—a total of about 15 grams—the ripple effects of the mailings extended far beyond those sickened or killed. Professor Leonard Cole of Rutgers University has estimated the total economic impact of the anthrax letter attacks at more than $6 billion. If only 15 grams of dry anthrax spores delivered by mail could produce such an enormous effect, the consequences of a large-scale aerosol release would be almost unimaginable.

As deadly as anthrax can be, it fortunately is not contagious. Because persons infected with the disease cannot transmit it to others, only those who are directly exposed to anthrax spores are at risk. Contagious diseases such as plague or smallpox, in contrast, can be transmitted through person-to-person contact, turning the initial set of victims into secondary sources of infection.

Many factors would affect the outcome of a biological attack, including the type and strain of agent; the time of day that it is released, and the prevailing wind, weather, and atmospheric conditions; and the basic health of the people who are exposed to it. Also important are the speed and manner in which public health authorities and medical professionals detect and respond to the resulting outbreak. A prompt response with effective medical countermeasures, such as antibiotics and vaccination, can potentially blunt the impact of an attack and thwart the terrorists' objectives.

The State Threat

During the Cold War, both the United States and the Soviet Union produced and stockpiled biological agents. But in November 1969, the Nixon administration renounced the U.S. offensive biological weapons program and then began to destroy its stockpile. This unilateral action opened the way to the successful negotiation of the 1972 Biological Weapons Convention (BWC), a multilateral treaty banning the development, production, and stockpiling of biological and toxin weapons.

Although the BWC was supposed to end all efforts by states to develop the capability to employ disease as a weapon, it has unfortunately failed to achieve this goal. Because the materials and equipment needed to produce biowarfare agents also have legitimate uses in scientific research and commercial industry, it is difficult to verify the BWC with any degree of confidence. A number of countries have secretly violated the treaty. The most egregious case was that of the Soviet Union, which created a massive biological weapons development and production complex employing more than 50,000 scientists and technicians.

Today, several important countries—Egypt, Israel, and Syria among them—remain outside the Biological Weapons Convention. The U.S.

State Department has also expressed concern that some parties to the treaty, such as Russia, China, North Korea, and Iran, may be pursuing offensive biological weapons programs in secret.

The Non-State Threat

States do not have a monopoly on biological weapons. In the past, a number of terrorist organizations and rogue individuals have sought to acquire and use biological or toxin agents. Such weapons may be attractive to terrorists because of their potential to inflict mass casualties or to be used covertly. In addition, as the anthrax letter attacks of autumn 2001 clearly demonstrated, even small-scale attacks of limited lethality can elicit a disproportionate amount of terror and social disruption.

The 2001 anthrax mailings were not the first incident of bioterrorism in the United States. In 1984, the Rajneeshees, a religious cult in Oregon, sought to reduce voter turnout and win control of the county government in an upcoming election by temporarily incapacitating local residents with a bacterial infection. In a test run of this scheme in September 1984, cult members contaminated 10 restaurant salad bars in a town in Oregon with salmonella, a common bacterium that causes food poisoning. The attack sickened 751 people, some seriously.

A decade later, members of a Japanese doomsday cult called Aum Shinrikyo released anthrax bacterial spores from the roof of a building in Tokyo. Fortunately, this attack failed because the cult produced and dispersed a harmless strain of anthrax that is used as a veterinary vaccine. Had Aum succeeded in acquiring a virulent strain and delivered it effectively, the casualties could have been in the thousands.

Islamist terrorist groups such as al Qaeda have also sought to acquire biological weapons in the past. Former CIA Director George Tenet wrote in his memoir that in 1999, in parallel with planning for the September 11 terrorist attacks, al Qaeda launched a concerted effort to develop an anthrax weapon that could inflict mass casualties. The group hired a Pakistani veterinarian named Rauf Ahmad to set up a bioweapons laboratory in Afghanistan, but he became disgruntled with the amount of money he was paid and eventually quit. To continue the anthrax work, al Qaeda then hired a Malaysian terrorist, Yazid Sufaat, who had studied biology at California State University in Sacramento. But in December 2001, after the U.S. invasion of Afghanistan,

Sufaat fled; he was captured by authorities as he tried to sneak back into Malaysia.

The cases of the Rajneeshees, Aum Shinrikyo, and al Qaeda underscore not only the dangerous potential of bioterrorism but also the technical difficulties that terrorist groups seeking such weapons are likely to encounter. Aum's failure to carry out a mass-casualty attack, despite its access to scientific expertise and ample financial resources, suggests that one should not oversimplify or exaggerate the threat of bioterrorism. Developing a biological weapon that can inflict mass casualties is an intricate undertaking, both technically and operationally complex.

Because of the difficulty of weaponizing and disseminating significant quantities of a biological agent in aerosol form, government officials and outside experts believe that no terrorist group currently has an operational capability to carry out a mass-casualty attack. But they could develop that capability quickly. In 2006 congressional testimony, Charles E. Allen, Under Secretary for Intelligence and Analysis at the Department of Homeland Security, noted that the threat of bioterrorism could increase rapidly if a terrorist group were able to recruit technical experts who had experience in a national biological warfare program, with knowledge comparable to that of the perpetrator of the 2001 anthrax letter attacks. In other words, given the high level of know-how needed to use disease as a weapon to cause mass casualties, the United States should be less concerned that terrorists will become biologists and far more concerned that biologists will become terrorists.

The last point bears repeating. We accept the validity of intelligence estimates about the current rudimentary nature of terrorist capabilities in the area of biological weapons but caution that the terrorists are trying to upgrade their capabilities and could do so by recruiting skilled scientists. In this respect the biological threat is greater than the nuclear; the acquisition of deadly pathogens, and their weaponization and dissemination in aerosol form, would entail fewer technical hurdles than the theft or production of weapons-grade uranium or plutonium and its assembly into an improvised nuclear device.

The difficulty of quantifying the bioterrorism threat to the United States does not make that threat any less real or compelling. It involves both motivation and capability, and the first ingredient is clearly present. Al Qaeda had an active biological weapons program in the past, and it is unlikely that the group has lost interest in employing infectious disease as a weapon. That roughly a half-dozen countries are suspected to possess or to be seeking biological weapons also provides ample grounds for concern.

The Future Threat

In addition to the current threat of bioweapons proliferation and terrorism, a set of over-the-horizon risks is emerging, associated with recent advances in the life sciences and biotechnology and the worldwide diffusion of these capabilities. Over the past few decades, scientists have gained a deep understanding of the structure of genetic material (DNA) and its role in directing the operation of living cells. This knowledge has led to remarkable gains in the treatment of disease and holds the promise of future medical breakthroughs. The industrial applications of this knowledge are also breathtaking: it is now possible to engineer microorganisms to give them new and beneficial characteristics.

Activity has been particularly intense in the area of biotechnology known as *synthetic genomics*. Since the early 1980s, scientists have developed automated machines that can synthesize long strands of DNA coding for genes and even entire microbial genomes. By piecing together large fragments of genetic material synthesized in the laboratory, scientists have been able to assemble infectious viruses, including the polio virus and the formerly extinct 1918 strain of the influenza virus, which was responsible for the global pandemic that killed between 20 million and 40 million people.

As DNA synthesis technology continues to advance at a rapid pace, it will soon become feasible to synthesize nearly any virus whose DNA sequence has been decoded—such as the smallpox virus, which was eradicated from nature in 1977—as well as artificial microbes that do not exist in nature. This growing ability to engineer life at the molecular level carries with it the risk of facilitating the development of new and more deadly biological weapons.

The only way to rule out the harmful use of advances in biotechnology would be to stifle their beneficial applications as well—and that is not a realistic option. Instead, the dual-use dilemma associated with the revolution in biology must be managed on an ongoing basis. As long as rapid innovations in biological science and the malevolent intentions of terrorists and proliferators continue on trajectories that are likely to intersect sooner or later, the risk that biological weapons pose to humanity must not be minimized or ignored.

Nuclear Risks

Pelindaba sprawls across the rolling hills west of Pretoria, a series of low, flat buildings among clusters of trees far greener than the brownish grasslands of the region. Its name is familiar to the citizens of South Africa, though few of them have ever seen it. It is known to be a repository of hundreds of kilograms of weapons-grade highly enriched uranium (HEU) that are the leftovers of the nuclear weapons program that produced six bombs before South Africa famously became the world's first and only nuclear nation to go the route of complete nuclear disarmament. It is also known as one of South Africa's most tightly secured installations, surrounded by 10,000-volt security fences, protected by a well-armed security force, and monitored by around-the-clock closed-circuit television cameras.

The attack came without warning, in the early morning hours of November 8, 2007.

Two armed teams struck the facility. The first consisted of four men: they burst into the facility's eastern block and headed for the control room. Later, authorities would say the four had gotten into the compound by cutting a hole in the high-voltage fence.

Inside the control room was the nuclear installation's emergency services operational officer and the control room's night shift supervisor. As the attackers burst in, the emergency services officer, Anton Gerber, pushed the control room supervisor under the desk—because she happened to be his fiancée and, he would later explain, he just wanted to protect her. The attackers shot him in the chest; the bullet, which narrowly missed his heart, broke a rib and punctured his lung—missing his spine by 2 centimeters, a doctor later said. Gerber said that after being shot, he continued trying to fight off the intruders as they attacked him with a screwdriver.

Then, as quickly as they had arrived, the intruders left—without making any effort to steal the nuclear material or sabotage the control room, the reactors, or anything else. They had grabbed one computer as they fled but dropped it when Pelindaba's security forces finally got to the scene, an estimated 45 minutes after the attackers had entered the compound. They got away cleanly. Later that night, a second team attacked. But guards spotted them early this time and sounded the alarm, and these attackers also fled.

South African authorities found the whole episode baffling—was this an inside caper with some sort of personal motive or was it really about nuclear terrorism? Why was it that the attackers spent 45 minutes inside the compound without being detected by either the high-tech equipment or the security guards?

International nuclear nonproliferation officials and nongovernmental experts found it frightening—focusing on what might have been. Could the attackers have stolen enough highly enriched uranium to fashion a nuclear bomb? Could South Africa's weapons-grade nuclear material have wound up in the possession of terrorists?

After reviewing the incident with South African authorities, the International Atomic Energy Agency (IAEA) determined that the HEU was never in any real danger, because the intruders never made it to the areas where the nuclear material was stored. Still, as Matthew Bunn, an associate professor of public policy at Harvard University, stated in his April 2008 testimony to the Senate Homeland Security and Governmental Affairs Committee, "This incident is nevertheless a potent reminder that inadequately secured nuclear material is a global problem, not one limited to the former Soviet Union."

So far as we know, the world has been the beneficiary of both skill and luck that terrorists have not yet obtained nuclear weapons-grade material and made it into a bomb. For nuclear thefts have occurred, as well as some well-known attempts by terrorists to buy bomb-making material on the black market.

o o o

The world today confronts a growing nuclear risk. Even as some states seek to acquire nuclear weapons, others are looking to expand their arsenals. Concern about the spread of nuclear weapons intensifies with the possibility of a large increase in nuclear power production to meet growing energy demands—a nuclear renaissance. As additional countries acquire nuclear facilities—particularly if they build uranium enrichment facilities or reprocessing facilities, ostensibly to provide fuel for their power plants and reduce the waste associated with the spent nuclear fuel—the number of states possessing the knowledge and capability to "breakout" and produce nuclear weapons will increase significantly. This also increases the risk that such materials could be diverted to, or stolen by, terrorist groups.

In addition, there is already a surfeit of nuclear material in the world. More than 40 countries possess nuclear material that could be used in a nuclear weapon, though at present almost all of it (about 95 percent) is in Russia and the United States. Hence those two countries have a special role to play in accounting for, securing, and reducing nuclear materials.

Most black market sources of actual weapons-grade nuclear material that terrorists seek appear to have originated from Russia or other former Soviet states. Much of it was most likely diverted or stolen by an individual with access to a facility designed to hold such materials. There have been multiple seizures by authorities in Russia and elsewhere of kilogram quantities of HEU. Even more disconcerting are reports that in 1998 the Russian Federal Security Service uncovered a plot by employees in a nuclear facility to steal 18.5 kilograms of material described only as suitable for the "production of components for nuclear weapons." Taken together these attempts represent enough material to produce at least one nuclear weapon.

More recently, there was a sting operation pulled off by the law enforcement officials of the Republic of Georgia. In February 2006, Georgian officials arrested Oleg Khintsagov, a Russian merchant from the North Ossetia region, on charges that he was trying to sell 100 grams of highly enriched uranium; they also took four Georgians into custody. After saying little publically about the case for a year, officials put out the word that the key to the arrest was a Georgian who spoke Turkish and pretended to be a Muslim from an organization interested in buying bomb-making fuel. Khintsagov claimed that he got the uranium from a source in the Siberian academic city of Novosibirsk. Russians said that their tests on the sample were inconclusive and expressed concerns that the arrest was politically motivated; Georgian officials said that the uranium appeared to be Russian. Khintsagov was sentenced to eight years in jail.

In another case, a small-time nuclear thief from Russia became a big-time nightmare for officials of the International Atomic Energy Agency.

Leonid Smirnov was a foreman at the Luch Scientific Production facility in Podolsk, just two hours by train from Moscow. His job was to weigh and inventory nuclear material, then dispense it to other workers. Because the scales at Luch were not very accurate, all measurements recorded for inventory were assumed to have a 3 percent margin of error. So, in the first years of the post-Soviet Russia, Smirnov figured that he would steal just a little bit at a time—always within the margin of error. And that's what he did. Night after night, he carried home a small amount of enriched uranium and put it in a lead-lined container that he kept on the balcony of his apartment, which overlooked a children's playground. In four months, he had collected 1,598 grams of 90-percent enriched uranium. Meanwhile, no discrepancies were visible in the ledgers at Luch.

Not being a practiced thief, Smirnov did not know how to sell it on the black market. When he sought advice from some friends who were thieves, they told him they were going to take the train to Moscow to sell some batteries; he could come along and bring his loot with him. But as it happened, the Podolsk police had been watching his pals and they were arrested. In the police station, after his friends were booked and led away, the police asked what he had in his lead container. Uranium, said Smirnov. The police ran out of the building into the street— and Smirnov ran after them, politely reassuring his captors and insisting that they were perfectly safe. He was arrested, and his helpfulness earned him a light sentence.

What led officials at IAEA to call Smirnov a nightmare was that he could have stolen enough material to make a bomb and sold it to terrorists—with the books at Luch still showing all the uranium accounted for and without IAEA officials ever having a clue that there was a problem.

This story underscores how U.S.-Russian cooperation can help secure so-called loose nukes—and that sometimes even small acts can lead to major improvements in security. Under the U.S. Cooperative Threat Reduction Program, also known as the Nunn-Lugar program (after its two respected congressional sponsors, Senators Sam Nunn and Richard Lugar), the United States paid for new digital state-of-the-art scales for the Luch facility. The result: no more rounding off within margins of error, and thus no more opportunities for small-time nuclear thieves like Leonid Smirnov to steal a bomb's worth of uranium, bit by bit.

∘ ∘ ∘

Unlike the uncertainties of a biological attack, which could occur silently and without being noticed for a number of days, a nuclear attack would be obvious, and most people understand the level of devastation and death it could cause. Still, it is instructive to review the damage that would follow a nuclear incident. Perhaps the best description has been provided by a member of our Commission, Graham Allison, director of the Belfer Center for Science and International Affairs at Harvard University, in his book *Nuclear Terrorism: The Ultimate Preventable Catastrophe* (2004).

Allison's scenarios:

> New York City—Al Qaeda rents a van, drives a Russian 10-kiloton nuclear bomb into Times Square, and detonates it. Times Square disappears instantly, as the heat from the blast would reach tens of millions of degrees Fahrenheit. The theater district, Grand Central Terminal, Rockefeller Center, Carnegie Hall, and Empire State Building would be gone, literally in a flash. Buildings further away, such as the United Nations Headquarters on the East River, the Flatiron Building, and the Metropolitan Museum would look like bombed-out shells. Half a million people who at noontime are in that half-mile radius of the blast site would be killed. Hundreds of thousands of others would die from collapsing buildings, fire, and fallout.

> San Francisco—A nuclear bomb is detonated in Union Square. Everything to the Museum of Modern Art would be vaporized. Massive destruction would exist from the Transamerica Building to Nob Hill.

> Chicago—A nuclear bomb explodes at Sears Tower. Everything from Navy Pier to the Eisenhower Expressway disappears. The United Center and Grant Park are destroyed. A firestorm sweeps from the White Sox's U.S. Cellular Field on the South Side to the Cubs' Wrigley Field on the North Side.

> Washington—A nuclear bomb at the Smithsonian Institution would destroy everything from the White House to the Capitol lawn. The Supreme Court would be rubble. The Pentagon, across the Potomac River, would be engulfed in flames.

∘ ∘ ∘

For all these reasons, our Commission joins the calls made by many others before us emphasizing the urgency of securing nuclear materials useful for weapons—right now, *before* they fall into the hands of terrorists.

At the same time, we cannot lose sight of concerns regarding the spread of nuclear weapons. Since the United States exploded the first nuclear bomb in 1945, seven additional states are known or suspected to have joined the nuclear weapons club: Russia, China, the United Kingdom, France, Israel, India, and Pakistan. In addition, South Africa built six nuclear weapons in the 1980s and dismantled them just before power was transferred to the post-apartheid government. North Korea conducted a nuclear weapons test in 2006, thus becoming the first country to have ratified the NPT and then break out of it by producing a nuclear weapon. In the past several years, the United States and Russia have significantly reduced their arsenals of nuclear weapons, while Pakistan, India, and China have been increasing their nuclear capabilities and reliance upon nuclear weapons in their strategic postures.

The emergence of this new kind of arms race in Asia raises the prospect of a nuclear war whose effects would be catastrophic both regionally and globally. Analysts estimate that a nuclear exchange between India and Pakistan that targets cities would kill millions of people and injure millions more. The risk of a nuclear war between the two neighbors is serious, given their ongoing dispute over Kashmir and the possibility that terrorist attacks by Pakistani militant groups might ignite a military confrontation.

Pakistan's nuclear weapons program is driven by its perception of the conventional and nuclear threat from India, while India's program is focused on both Pakistan and China. China is also fueling the arms race, both by increasing its own strategic forces and by not stopping Chinese entities from supporting Pakistan's strategic programs. At present, all three are expanding their nuclear arsenals with no clear end in sight.

At the same time, nuclear developments in Iran, North Korea, and Syria are also disturbing, because they represent a possible tipping point toward cascading nuclear proliferation. The continued production and testing of nuclear weapons by North Korea could provoke Japan or South Korea to reconsider its nuclear postures. Similarly, Iran's continued pursuit of a fissile material production capability, combined with the recent revelation that Syria was constructing a plutonium production reactor with North Korean assistance, increases the pressure on Saudi Arabia, Egypt, and other states in the region to pursue their own programs. In this context, increased U.S., French, Russian, and Chinese contributions to civilian nuclear programs in the Middle East and South Asia are potentially destabilizing, if not managed properly.

The path leading to proliferation apparently was not difficult to follow. Some states pursued the development of nuclear technologies and capabilities within their own borders, and some relied on direct state-to-state transfers. Others employed espionage to acquire the technology and knowledge they needed, and still others relied on independent, illicit procurement agents to acquire nuclear technology that was mainly dual-use from other weapons and civil nuclear programs. Some benefited from the marketing of nuclear technology and expertise by scientists from other state programs. Most used a combination of these methods as they tried to achieve their goal.

Several states have tapped into black markets and illicit networks that supply nuclear materials, designs, and expertise to almost any buyer who is interested. The best known of these networks, run by the Pakistani scientist A. Q. Khan, assisted Iran, Libya, North Korea, and perhaps others in acquiring the technologies and designs needed to develop illicit nuclear programs. It unraveled in 2003 after authorities intercepted the BBC *China*, a cargo ship on its way to Libya with gas centrifuge components on board. It is unlikely that Khan's network could be reconstituted, but black-marketing of dangerous technologies, designs, and expertise continues to this day and is a major concern.

The recent discovery that North Korea provided Syria with a nuclear reactor for plutonium production escalates existing concerns about future nuclear proliferation. North Korea, after all, has already sold nuclear weapons–capable ballistic missiles to Pakistan, Iran, and several other states in the Middle East.

Nonetheless, past decisions by other countries may offer some hope for U.S. and international nonproliferation efforts. Belarus, Kazakhstan, and Ukraine agreed to the removal of nuclear weapons from their territory after the fall of the Soviet Union, and South Africa agreed to give up its nuclear weapons in 1991. Taiwan, South Korea, Argentina, Brazil, and Libya formerly had nuclear weapons programs but have reversed course. An additional 20 countries that at one time considered building nuclear weapons ultimately subscribed to norms of nonproliferation. But even when countries give up their nuclear weapons programs, there is still a risk that their nuclear know-how and materials will fall into the hands of terrorists or others.

At the moment, al Qaeda is judged to be the sole terrorist group actively intent on conducting a nuclear attack against the United States. For the foreseeable future, no extremists or groups to which they belong will be able on their own to produce nuclear weapons–usable materials. As a result, terrorists can successfully employ a nuclear device only if they acquire a weapon or weapons-usable materials from a state nuclear program. It is therefore imperative that authorities secure nuclear weapons and materials at their source.

Al Qaeda began its efforts to acquire nuclear weapons–usable material in the early 1990s. While bin Laden was living in Sudan, his aides received word that a Sudanese military officer was offering to sell weapons-grade uranium. Bin Laden was willing to pay full price for the material: $1.5 million. After the purchase, however, the al Qaeda members realized that they had been scammed. This failure apparently did not discourage bin Laden—and his persistence highlights the seriousness of his interest. In the spring of 2001, bin Laden met with a Pakistani former nuclear scientist, Bashiruddin Mahmood, and discussed the development of nuclear and other weapons of mass destruction.

Today, all of this still points to intent but not capability. U.S. government officials and recognized experts have testified that al Qaeda probably does not currently have the nuclear materials or the technical expertise necessary to produce a nuclear weapon. However, they also recognize that the terrorists' ability to produce such a device could increase dramatically should they recruit just one or two individuals with access to nuclear materials or with knowledge of nuclear weapons designs.

TWO
Findings and Recommendations

Biological Proliferation and Terrorism

Only a thin wall of terrorist ignorance and inexperience now protects us.
—Former Secretary of the Navy Richard Danzig

Biological science and technology today transcend borders. These fields engage a vast and expanding array of actors in the government, private, and commercial sectors, and they are advancing at a remarkable pace. The more that sophisticated capabilities, including genetic engineering and gene synthesis, spread around the globe, the greater the potential that terrorists will use them to develop biological weapons. The challenge for U.S. policymakers is to prevent that potential from becoming a reality by keeping dangerous pathogens—and the equipment, technology, and know-how needed to weaponize them—out of the hands of criminals, terrorists, and proliferant states.

The Commission believes that much more can be done to prevent biological weapons (BW) proliferation and terrorism—even as we recognize it is unrealistic to think that we can completely eliminate the possibility of misuse. Accordingly, we recommend a number of initiatives to enhance efforts at prevention, in addition to existing programs by the Department of Health and Human Services and the Department of Homeland Security to mitigate the consequences of a biological weapons attack.

Consistent with its legislative mandate, this Commission has focused on assessing and making recommendations on how to improve measures for the prevention of biological proliferation and terrorism. Nevertheless, countering the threat of BW proliferation and terrorism will require concerted action across a policy continuum that extends from prevention to consequence management. Prevention alone is not sufficient, and a robust system for public health preparedness and response is vital to the nation's security. In order to deter biological attacks, we need to demonstrate—through effective preparedness measures and public exercises—that we are capable of blunting the impact of an attack and thus thwarting the terrorists' objectives.

To date, the U.S. government has invested most of its nonproliferation efforts and diplomatic capital in preventing nuclear terrorism. The Commission believes that it should make the more likely threat—bioterrorism—a higher priority. Only by elevating the priority of the biological weapons threat will it be possible to bring about substantial improvements in global biosecurity. To this end, the new administration should urgently develop a comprehensive approach to the prevention of biological proliferation and terrorism.

Domestic Findings and Recommendation

Securing Dangerous Pathogens

A major hurdle for terrorists seeking biological weapons is the difficulty of acquiring disease-causing microbes (chiefly bacteria and viruses) and toxins (poisonous substances produced by living creatures) that can be harnessed to incapacitate or kill humans, livestock, or crops. Although dangerous pathogens such as the anthrax bacterium can be isolated from natural sources, it would generally be easier for terrorists to steal or divert well-characterized "hot" strains from a research laboratory or culture collection.

To reduce the likelihood of theft or diversion, in 1996 Congress created the Select Agent Program, which established a list of pathogens and toxins of bioterrorism concern. The initial regulations required the reporting of all transfers of these "select agents" to other laboratories and mandated that the facilities involved in the transfers be registered with the Department of Health and Human Services (HHS) or the Department of Agriculture (USDA).

In 2002, in response to the anthrax letter attacks of autumn 2001, Congress expanded the list of select agents and added a requirement that all U.S. laboratories that possess or transfer select agents must register with one of the two departments. In addition, all such laboratories must implement enhanced security measures including physical access controls and the FBI vetting of all scientists, technicians, and laboratory officials before they are allowed to work with select agents. Biodefense researchers at U.S. Army laboratories must submit to a more stringent vetting process that includes a background investigation and a security clearance. Nevertheless, in August 2008, the Department of Justice identified Bruce E. Ivins, a U.S. Army researcher, as the sole perpetrator of the 2001 anthrax letter attacks, a development that has raised questions about the adequacy of current personnel vetting procedures.

Since the 2001 terrorist attacks on the United States, the Departments of Defense, Health and Human Services, Homeland Security, and other agencies have spent or allocated nearly $50 billion for civilian biodefense. This huge influx of funding has been accompanied by the design and construction of numerous federal, state, and private high-containment laboratories (at Biosafety Level 3), as well as maximum-containment laboratories (at Biosafety Level 4), that work with the most dangerous pathogens. For example, the number of Biosafety Level 4 (BSL-4) labs is expected to triple from 5 in 2001 to 15 in 2012. This rapid expansion of laboratory capacity has been justified by the need for research on measures to counter both deliberate acts of bioterrorism and the global spread of emerging infectious diseases of natural origin, such as SARS (severe acute respiratory syndrome) and avian influenza.

At the same time, the dramatic increase in the number of high-containment labs in the absence of a comprehensive regulatory framework has raised safety, security, and terrorism concerns. At present, some 400 research facilities in the United States are authorized to store and handle select agents, and nearly 15,000 individuals have been approved to work with them. The rapid growth in the number of facilities and people handling select agents has increased the risk of laboratory accidents or intentional misuse by insiders. Moreover, no single entity in the executive branch is responsible for overseeing and managing the risks associated with all the high-containment (BSL-3) laboratories operated by the U.S. government, industry, or academia.

Promoting a Biosecurity Culture

The government and the private sector must urgently address both *biosafety* concerns (preventing the accidental infection of laboratory workers and the release into the environment of dangerous pathogens) and *biosecurity* concerns (preventing the theft or diversion of dangerous pathogens for nefarious purposes).

The nuclear age began with a mushroom cloud—and all those who worked in the nuclear industry in any capacity, military or civilian, instantly understood that they must work and live under a clear and undeniable security mandate. But the life sciences community has never experienced a comparable iconic event to focus their attention on security. Instead, most biologists view their research as an absolute good that promotes human health and prosperity, and they jealously guard their independence. There is understandable tension between the biology community and the government with regard to regulatory and oversight efforts, such as the Select Agent Rules. Although the recent assertion that a U.S. Army scientist was responsible for the anthrax letter attacks has created some awareness of the need for greater security, much still remains to be accomplished.

The choice is stark. The life sciences community can wait until a catastrophic biological attack occurs before it steps up to its security responsibilities. Or it can act proactively in its own enlightened self-interest, aware that the reaction of the political system to a major bioterrorist event would likely be extreme and even draconian, resulting in significant harm to the scientific enterprise.

Because science is a global activity, any biosecurity regime must ultimately be international in nature. As a first step, it is necessary for the United States to put its own house in order and lead the rest of the world by providing the highest standards of biosafety and biosecurity. The U.S. goal must be to keep dual-use materials, technology, and expertise out of the hands of terrorists and proliferators.

The U.S. government has sought to foster the development of a "culture of security awareness" within the life sciences community to prevent the misuse of biology for warfare or terrorism. However, scientists in academia and industry generally view the Select Agent Program as an unnecessary burden rather than as an important means of preventing bioterrorism. To help change this attitude, federal agencies have launched a number of outreach and education efforts.

In 2005, the FBI established the Science and Technology Outreach Program (since renamed the Biological Sciences Outreach Program) to increase its dialogue with the academic, biotechnology, and public health communities and thereby gain their aid in thwarting bioterrorists. That same year, the Bureau established the National Security Higher Education Advisory Board, which consists of about 20 presidents of major U.S. research universities. The advisory board aims to promote communication between the U.S. government and academic leaders on issues related to homeland security, law enforcement, and visa and immigration policies.

Meanwhile, in 2004, the Department of Health and Human Services created the National Science Advisory Board for Biosecurity to consider how to minimize the risk that advances in bioscience and biotechnology could be misused to threaten public health and national security. This committee is developing guidelines to improve the oversight of biological research.

Microbial Forensics

Microbial forensics is a new science that involves the use of molecular tools, such as DNA sequencing and isotopic analysis, to analyze a microbial pathogen or toxin. Such techniques can help determine the source of a particular strain of pathogen, thereby providing useful investigative leads. When combined with more traditional techniques, such as the analysis of hair, fibers, and fingerprints, microbial forensics can narrow the range of suspects in a bioterror attack. The FBI investigation into the anthrax-tainted letters of autumn 2001 provided a strong impetus for the rapid development of this new field. Analysis of subtle variations in the DNA sequences of different anthrax bacterial strains ultimately made it possible to pinpoint the source of the material used in the 2001 attacks to a single flask at the U.S. Army's biodefense research center at Fort Detrick, in Maryland.

A number of U.S. government agencies are currently involved in microbial forensics. In partnership with the FBI, the Department of Homeland Security's Science and Technology Directorate operates the National Bioforensic Analysis Center, which President George W. Bush designated in 2004 as the lead federal facility to conduct and facilitate the technical forensic analysis and interpretation of materials from biocrime and bioterror investigations.

RECOMMENDATION 1: The United States should undertake a series of mutually reinforcing domestic measures to prevent bioterrorism: (1) conduct a comprehensive review of the domestic program to secure dangerous pathogens, (2) develop a national strategy for advancing bioforensic capabilities, (3) tighten government oversight of high-containment laborato-

ries, (4) promote a culture of security awareness in the life sciences community, and (5) enhance the nation's capabilities for rapid response to prevent biological attacks from inflicting mass casualties.

The Commission believes there are a number of specific actions that the United States should undertake to implement this recommendation.

ACTION: The Department of Health and Human Services should lead an interagency review of the domestic program to secure dangerous pathogens.

Congress passed legislation in 2002 strengthening the Select Agent Program, which had been established to secure dangerous pathogens used in research laboratories. But since the tightened regulations have gone into effect, the U.S. government has not conducted an internal review of the program's effectiveness in improving biological security and its impact on legitimate scientific research. A representative of a leading professional association in the life sciences expressed to the Commission the concerns of some of its members, who feel that the Select Agent Program is impeding collaboration with foreign scientists and blocking transfers of endemic pathogens from developing countries for study in U.S. laboratories. Although the Centers for Disease Control and Prevention (CDC) recently commissioned the Homeland Security Institute to review some aspects of the Select Agent Program, this effort is too narrow in scope and does not include the full set of stakeholders.

The Commission believes that an interagency review of the implementation of the Select Agent Program is long overdue. Issues or concerns emerging from such a review should be addressed during the first year of the new administration. The review should explore ways of implementing the Select Agent Program so that it continues to prevent the misuse of dangerous pathogens without hampering vital domestic research and international collaboration.

ACTION: The Department of Homeland Security should take the lead in developing a national strategy for advancing microbial forensics capabilities.

Microbial forensics, a set of genetic and physical techniques for analyzing a biological or toxin agent that has been acquired by a proliferant state or terrorist group, can clarify where a breach in laboratory security has occurred. It can also help identify the perpetrators of a biological weapons attack and support their criminal prosecution. For deterrence, defense, and law enforcement purposes, the U.S. government is currently making a concerted effort to increase the likelihood that biological materials that have been obtained illicitly or used in an attack can be traced back to their source and perhaps linked to a terrorist organization or its state sponsor.

The Commission supports these efforts but believes they are not sufficient. By the end of 2009, the U.S. government must develop a national strategy for acquiring a state-of-the-art capability for microbial forensics. Such a national strategy should (1) facilitate the development and maintenance of a comprehensive library of pathogen reference strains; (2) establish a government-wide set of standard procedures for collecting, processing, and analyzing samples to improve consistency and quality, and identify both a lead agency to direct this effort and the roles and responsibilities of support agencies; and (3) fund basic research to support the further development of microbial forensic techniques.

ACTION: The Department of Health and Human Services, in coordination with the Department of Homeland Security, should lead an interagency effort to tighten government oversight of high-containment laboratories.

Despite the inherent safety and security risks associated with high-containment laboratories, such facilities in the United States are not specifically regulated; they become subject to federal oversight only if they are government-funded or possess pathogens and toxins on the Select Agent List. Thus many BSL-3 laboratories that work with dangerous but unlisted pathogens, such as the SARS virus, operate outside of federal regulation and indeed even federal knowledge of their existence. Moreover, the number of scientists working with dangerous pathogens is increasing—and many are working with them for the first time. These changes have led to a higher incidence of accidents and laboratory-acquired infections and to new biosecurity concerns.

The problems have been exacerbated by the unbridled growth in the number of high-containment laboratories since 2001, which has occurred without effective and coordinated federal oversight. In October 2007, the Government Accountability Office underscored this deficiency, reporting that "no single federal agency has the mission and, therefore, is accountable for tracking the number of all BSL-3 and BSL-4 labs within the United States. . . . Therefore, no agency is responsible for determining the aggregate risks associated with the expansion of these labs."

The Commission believes that safety and security considerations warrant direct federal oversight of all high-containment laboratories. We recommend that the next administration take appropriate action to (1) determine present and future requirements for research on biodefense threats and emerging infectious diseases, and plan future expansion to minimize the associated safety and security risks; (2) require federal registration of all BSL-3 and BSL-4 facilities (whether or not they work with select agents), identify a lead federal agency to oversee and enforce the registration process, and create a government-wide database of all high-containment labs in the United States; (3) implement a common set of safety and security requirements for all high-containment labs; and (4) mandate standard biosafety and biosecurity training for all personnel who work in high-containment labs, and fund the development of educational materials for that purpose.

The new administration should act immediately to complete its assessment of national requirements for high-containment laboratories and take the action necessary to establish federal oversight of all BSL-3 and BSL-4 laboratories in the United States. The government should also consider centralizing the regulatory functions for biosafety and biosecurity by developing a new oversight mechanism for high-containment laboratories that combines the existing CDC/USDA Select Agent Program and the National Institutes of Health Guidelines for Research Involving Recombinant DNA Molecules.

ACTION: The Department of Health and Human Services and Congress should promote a culture of security awareness in the life sciences community.

Members of the life sciences community—universities, medical and veterinary schools, nongovernmental biomedical research institutes, trade associations, and biotechnology and pharmaceutical companies—must foster a bottom-up effort to sensitize researchers to biosecurity issues and concerns. Scientists should understand the ethical imperative to "do no harm," strive to anticipate the potential consequences of their research, and design and conduct experiments in a way that minimizes safety and security risks.

At present, no clear procedures, structures, or support systems exist for addressing the problem of dual-use research in the life sciences. The next administration should create a domestic review and oversight system for such research. The Commission also calls on the leaders of the life sciences community, both inside and outside of government, to speak out clearly and frequently about the professional responsibility of scientists to prevent the misuse of biology for hostile purposes. Congress should hold hearings to discuss the problem and should foster practical solutions for addressing it.

Several other bottom-up steps are also warranted. The currently separate concepts of biosafety and biosecurity should be combined into a unified conceptual framework of *laboratory risk management*. This framework should be integrated into a program of mandatory education and training for scientists and technicians in the life sciences field, whether they are working in the academy or in industry. Such training should begin with advanced college and graduate students and extend to career scientists. The U.S. government should also fund the development of educational materials and reference manuals on biosafety and biosecurity issues. At the same time, the responsibilities of laboratory biosafety officers should be expanded to include laboratory security and oversight of select agents, and all biosafety officers should be tested and certified by a competent government authority.

Finally, whistleblower mechanisms should be established within the professional life sciences community so that scientists can report— without risk of retaliation—their concerns about safety and security, including suspicious or aberrant behavior on the part of colleagues. For example, a help line might be established under the auspices of a nongovernmental or professional organization that would receive reports from scientists about suspicious activities and then initiate investigative action when appropriate.

Findings and Recommendations

ACTION: The Department of Health and Human Services, in coordination with the Department of Homeland Security, should take steps to enhance the nation's capacity for rapid response to prevent an anthrax attack from inflicting mass casualties.

Since 2001, the U.S. government has taken important steps to prepare a national response to a bioterrorist attack involving anthrax bacterial spores, the most likely near-term biological threat to the United States. Because the risk of bioterrorists' using anthrax is real and the timeline for responding to an attack is extremely unforgiving, the United States must make a concerted effort to improve its capabilities in this area. Although our mandate is to examine preventive measures, the Commission believes that a substantially greater effort is needed to develop and make operational a response plan that can counter an anthrax attack effectively. This plan would also help deter such an attack by significantly reducing its probability of success. Establishing an effective system to respond to an anthrax attack would also improve the nation's ability to manage other public health disasters, be they natural or man-made.

Inhalational anthrax can be prevented in exposed individuals if effective oral antibiotics are administered during the first 48 hours after infection—before the onset of acute symptoms, when the disease becomes highly lethal and difficult to treat. Although the Department of Health and Human Services has maintained a national stockpile of medical countermeasures since 1999, distributing these items during a national emergency remains a major challenge. In the case of inhalational anthrax, the 48-hour window imposes an extremely demanding timeline for executing an effective medical response: the U.S. government must detect an aerosol attack soon after it occurs, immediately set the response plan in motion, and distribute stockpiled antibiotics to the affected states, which in turn must dispense them to the local population—all within two days.

In October 2008, Health and Human Services Secretary Michael Leavitt announced that his department is working with the U.S. Postal Service to assist state and local authorities in addressing the distribution problem. In the event of an anthrax attack, mail carriers, escorted by police officers, would quickly deliver a short-term supply of antibiotics from the national stockpile to all residences in the affected area, giving state and local public health authorities enough time to set up dispensing centers for longer-term (60-day) antibiotic treatment. We have not had time to review this new initiative but are inclined to doubt that it fully satisfies this vital need. The United States still does not have and must quickly develop a fully comprehensive and tested system for the rapid delivery of lifesaving medical countermeasures against anthrax and other bioterrorist threats.

As a first step in addressing these issues, the Bush administration submitted a fiscal year 2009 budget amendment request asking Congress for an additional $969 million to fund the development and manufacture of medical countermeasures, innovative approaches to distribution and decontamination, and upgrades to the BioWatch network of air samplers designed to permit early detection of a bioterrorist attack. These urgent funding requirements should be taken up early in the next Congress. In addition, the next administration should, as a matter of national priority, fully implement an effective anthrax preparedness strategy.

The Commission believes that an innovative approach will be needed to solve the problem of how to rapidly dispense antibiotics and other medical countermeasures to the exposed population should a large-scale bioterrorist attack occur. Serious consideration should be given to harnessing the existing distribution networks of large retail stores and forging effective public-private partnerships. Furthermore, the dispensing system for medical countermeasures should be exercised and reviewed regularly to demonstrate both to the American public and to our enemies that the U.S. government takes the threat of bioterrorism seriously and is fully prepared to defend the population. "Red-teaming" exercises, in which deliberate attempts are made to disrupt the dispensing system, are also useful for identifying areas of weakness. These exercises should assess the emergency response and treatment capabilities of hospitals as well as the effectiveness of public health networks for gathering and evaluating hospital reports of infectious disease cases.

Another potential gap in U.S. biological defenses is the threat of bioterrorist attacks with strains of anthrax that have been genetically modified to make them resistant to standard antibiotics. Given this potential threat, additional funding is needed for the National Institutes of Health and the private sector to develop new classes of antibiotics, as well as antitoxin treatments that can neutralize the deadly toxins released by the anthrax bacterium in an infected individual.

Finally, an effective public information strategy is essential to educate and inform the U.S. population during a bioterrorist attack, so that citizens are able to take effective action to minimize their risk of exposure, prevent the person-to-person spread of contagious agents, and diagnose and treat themselves and their loved ones at home when possible so that hospitals and other treatment centers are not inundated. Such a public information strategy was sorely lacking during the 2001 anthrax letter attacks. The Department of Health and Human Services and Department of Homeland Security, in cooperation with state and local health departments and emergency responders, should prepare specific messages that can be disseminated after a bioterrorist attack to facilitate citizens' self-protection and self-decontamination.

International Findings and Recommendation

Biological Weapons Convention

The cornerstone of international efforts to prevent biological weapons proliferation and terrorism is the 1972 Biological Weapons Convention (BWC). This treaty bans the development, production, and acquisition of biological and toxin weapons and the delivery systems specifically designed for their dispersal. The BWC forbids member states (now numbering more than 160) from assisting other governments, non-state entities, or individuals in obtaining biological weapons. In addition, the convention requires each state party to take "any necessary measures to prohibit and prevent" the activities banned by the treaty on its territory and other areas under its jurisdiction and control. This provision has been interpreted as obligating each member state to adopt domestic legislation imposing criminal sanctions on its citizens for developing or producing biological weapons, and to secure dangerous pathogens from unauthorized access or theft. Although the negotiation of the BWC was a major achievement of arms control, the treaty has been marred by serious violations and a lack of universal membership.

Unlike many other arms control treaties, the BWC does not contain any formal verification mechanisms, nor does it establish an international implementing organization. The treaty was negotiated at the height of the Cold War, when the Soviet Union refused in principle to accept any on-site arms control measures, leaving bilateral consultations or an investigation by the United Nations Security Council as the only avenues for addressing concerns about noncompliance. In fact, violations of the BWC are extraordinarily difficult to verify. Because biological activities, materials, and equipment can be used for good as well as harm, compliance ultimately depends on the underlying intent, which may be peaceful or offensive. Yet evidence for the intent to use biology as a weapon is hard to discern: nefarious purposes can easily be concealed within a host of legitimate activities, such as pharmaceutical development, vaccine production, and general life sciences research.

Despite these serious verification challenges, the perceived weakness of the Biological Weapons Convention prompted many countries in the early 1990s to call for the negotiation of a legally binding verification regime to supplement the convention. The U.S. government under President George H. W. Bush opposed this proposal, arguing that because biotechnology is essentially dual-use, effective verification of the convention by an international regime was impossible. In 1994, however, the Clinton administration sidestepped the verification issue and decided to support the negotiation of a protocol to the BWC as a means of promoting greater transparency and of deterring noncompliance.

International negotiations began in Geneva in 1995, but major disagreements soon emerged. Russia, still suspected of harboring an illicit biological weapons program and apparently seeking to limit the prohibitions of the BWC, insisted that key terms in the convention be defined narrowly. Iran, China, Pakistan, India, and other members of the Non-Aligned Movement demanded that the protocol end all national export controls, on the grounds that such controls "discriminated" against developing countries. Finally, the European Union and others pressed for intrusive inspections that went much further than U.S. proposals for greater transparency, raising both national security and commercial concerns that sensitive information might be compromised.

In mid-2001, after more than six years of talks and the introduction of a compromise text by the chairman of the negotiating forum, the United States withdrew its support for the draft Biological Weapons Convention Protocol, prompting widespread international criticism. The United States concluded that the confidence-building transparency sought by the protocol could be achieved only at the unacceptable cost of (1) creating the false perception that the convention was verifiable by an international organization, (2) acquiescing to an international inspection regime that could jeopardize sensitive U.S. information, and (3) accepting Russian and Non-Aligned Movement demands that would have seriously undermined international biological weapons nonproliferation efforts and the convention itself. These concerns remain valid today, when the continuing global spread of dual-use biological materials, equipment, and facilities has only made verifying compliance to the BWC more difficult.

In 2002, at the convention's fifth review conference, the member states agreed to suspend the protocol negotiations indefinitely. Instead, they adopted a U.S. proposal to hold a series of annual expert and political meetings between the review conferences held every five years. Launched in 2003, these annual meetings have focused on the prevention of bioterrorism by addressing such topics as domestic legislation implementing the BWC, pathogen and laboratory security, infectious disease detection and response, scientific codes of conduct, and investigations of alleged use of biological weapons. The annual meetings have proven useful for increasing international awareness of biological security issues, and the Sixth Review Conference in 2006 renewed the intersessional work program until the next review conference in 2011.

Biological Threat Reduction

Cooperative threat reduction (CTR) is a series of U.S. government programs that were originally designed to secure and dismantle WMD stockpiles from the former Soviet Union (FSU). U.S. biological CTR efforts in Russia and the former Soviet republics have focused on three objectives: (1) dismantling former biological weapons production facilities, (2) improving the security of collections of dangerous pathogens, and (3) engaging former biological weapons scientists and redirecting them into peaceful areas of research. In recent years, the United States has sharply cut back its biological CTR programs in Russia because of bureaucratic and political difficulties in dealing with the Russian government, which has refused U.S. requests for greater transparency at former biological weapons facilities controlled by the Ministry of Defense.

The U.S. government is also pursuing biosecurity cooperation and engagement outside the former Soviet Union. The Biosecurity Engagement Program, launched in 2006 by the State Department, seeks to promote pathogen security and collaborative bioscience research in critical regions of the world. The objective of the program is to promote legitimate bioscience research in select countries while addressing their dangerous blend of bioterrorism threats, emerging infectious diseases, poorly secured collections of dangerous pathogens, and rapidly expanding biotechnology industries. Initially it is focusing on countries in South Asia, Southeast Asia, and the Middle East that have indigenous terrorist groups interested in acquiring biological weapons. Pilot efforts in Indonesia and the Philippines include conducting risk assessments; developing country-level strategies for bilateral engagement on laboratory biosafety, pathogen security, and the monitoring of outbreaks of infectious disease; and developing a grants assistance program to promote research collaboration between U.S. and local institutions. This effort must be expanded to additional regions.

Global Monitoring of Infectious Disease Outbreaks

Crucial to mounting a defense against biological weapons development and attack is the early detection and reporting of outbreaks of infectious disease, a capability known as *disease surveillance*. Today, a number of surveillance networks provide early warning of outbreaks throughout the world. Although these networks are designed primarily to detect naturally occurring infections such as SARS, Ebola, West Nile virus, and avian influenza, they could also detect deliberate attacks using biological weapons.

The World Health Organization (WHO) is the focal point of international disease surveillance efforts. The WHO's International Health Regulations (IHR) require participating states to notify the WHO of a potential "public health emergency of international concern" so that an epidemic can be contained before it spreads across borders. The regulations also require WHO member states to meet specified benchmarks for national disease surveillance and response capabilities. In addition, an operations center at WHO Headquarters is responsible for integrating the outbreak reports it receives from member states into the Global Outbreak Alert and Response Network and dispatching response teams from approximately 150 partner organizations around the globe with the goal of containing disease outbreaks close to where they originate. Disease surveillance and reporting remains a difficult and demanding task, however, and outbreak information is not always provided by WHO member states on a timely basis.

Findings and Recommendations

Today's international surveillance networks are not comprehensive in their coverage, and belated detection of an outbreak hinders a swift response. Reporting delays may result from political or bureaucratic hurdles as well as the lengthy laboratory analyses needed to confirm a disease diagnosis. Another problem is that many infectious diseases are zoonotic—that is, they infect both animals and people. In such natural infections as West Nile virus and avian influenza, wild birds are sentinel species: they typically become infected before humans and provide early warning of an impending epidemic. Similar sentinels may exist for zoonotic diseases that pose bioterrorism concerns, including anthrax, tularemia, plague, Q fever, Venezuelan equine encephalitis, rabies, and viral hemorrhagic fevers. Yet surveillance systems for animal diseases are significantly less developed than those for human diseases, and WHO and the World Organization for Animal Health (OIE) have not fully integrated their respective disease surveillance networks.

RECOMMENDATION 2: The United States should undertake a series of mutually reinforcing measures at the international level to prevent biological weapons proliferation and terrorism: (1) press for an international conference of countries with major biotechnology industries to promote biosecurity, (2) conduct a global assessment of biosecurity risks, (3) strengthen global disease surveillance networks, and (4) propose a new action plan for achieving universal adherence to and effective national implementation of the Biological Weapons Convention, for adoption at the next review conference in 2011.

Ensuring that the life sciences evolve safely and securely will require both top-down oversight by national governments and bottom-up leadership from all the life sciences communities—professional, academic, and industry. National regulation and international cooperation are necessary elements of a global biosecurity framework, and can help countries meet their obligations under UN Security Council Resolution 1540 to prevent terrorist groups from acquiring access to biological weapons and the materials and equipment needed to produce them. Ultimately, however, governments can only point the way—those working in the life sciences must commit to the journey.

ACTION: The Department of State and Department of Health and Human Services should press for an international conference of countries with major biotechnology industries to discuss the norms and safeguards necessary to keep dangerous pathogens out of the hands of terrorists and to ensure that the global revolution in the life sciences unfolds safely and securely.

With a view to achieving broad international involvement in and support for biosecurity, the Commission believes that the United States should press for the establishment of an international conference of countries, bringing together Western industrialized states that possess advanced capabilities in the life sciences (e.g., Canada, France, Germany, Japan, Switzerland, the United Kingdom, and the United States) and emerging biotech powers (e.g., Brazil, China, India, Malaysia, Singapore, South Africa, South Korea, and Russia) to develop a road map for ensuring that the revolution in biology unfolds safely and securely.

The purpose of such a biotech powers conference should be to identify key principles of biosecurity, to harmonize national regulatory frameworks for dangerous pathogens and dual-use research of concern, and to promote international biosecurity cooperation. Furthermore, the conference would consider bottom-up approaches for raising the awareness of life scientists in academic institutions and commercial enterprises about the security dimensions of their work, with a view to creating a transnational "culture of security awareness." Once consensus on a biosecurity road map has been reached, it could serve as the basis for broader regional and international engagement and consensus building of the kind required to devise an effective global framework.

ACTION: The Department of State should lead a global assessment of biological threats and engage in targeted biological threat prevention programs in additional countries.

The Commission recommends that the Department of State lead a comprehensive effort to prevent the emergence of new biological threats, as well as reduce existing threats. This initiative, which might be termed the Cooperative Bio-Threat Prevention Program, would involve the following steps: (1) conduct a global assessment of pathogen security, (2) develop a prioritized list of countries where poorly secured collections of dangerous pathogens are at risk of theft or diversion, and (3) devise a comprehensive strategy for assisting these countries to upgrade the security of their laboratories and their culture collections. Supporting this type of global approach to biological threat prevention, which should be integrated with efforts to improve the public health infrastructure in the affected countries, will require increased funding.

ACTION: The Department of Health and Human Services (primarily through the Centers for Disease Control and Prevention) should work to strengthen global disease surveillance networks.

Global networks for infectious disease surveillance can provide an "extended defense perimeter" for the United States by making it possible to detect and contain outbreaks of contagious diseases, whether natural or human-caused, before they reach U.S. shores. Such networks can also help defend U.S. military bases, embassies, and other American interests abroad against such outbreaks.

The Commission believes that more can and should be done, both domestically and internationally, to enhance the health security of the U.S. population by improving infectious disease surveillance and reporting capabilities. The gaps between the medical, public health, veterinary, and wildlife health communities must be closed to create integrated reporting systems for disease outbreaks in humans and animals, as well as effective response capabilities. Internationally, the United States should assist the World Organization for Animal Health (OIE) to improve its capabilities for monitoring outbreaks of zoonotic diseases, and should facilitate the integration of data and analyses between the WHO and the OIE.

Complementing the efforts of international organizations, the United States should continue to foster the development of other global surveillance networks. The Global Disease Surveillance System, sponsored by the Centers for Disease Control and Prevention, has significant promise and should be further developed and expanded to ensure worldwide coverage. In addition, the United States should offer bilateral assistance to those developing countries at greatest risk of epidemics, helping them to establish surveillance networks for detecting and reporting both human and animal disease outbreaks prior to a confirmed laboratory diagnosis. In order to promote these and other biosecurity efforts, the Department of Health and Human Services should strengthen the capabilities of its Office of the Secretary, better positioning it to lead international engagement programs. Finally, the department should encourage disease surveillance programs undertaken by nongovernmental organizations.

ACTION: The United States should reaffirm the critical importance of the 1972 Biological Weapons Convention to international peace and security by proposing a new action plan for achieving universal adherence and effective national implementation, to be adopted at the next review conference in 2011.

The 1972 Biological Weapons Convention constitutes a standard of international conduct that should be universally supported. It outlaws biological weapons, bars parties to it from providing assistance to anyone seeking such weapons, and obligates them to take "any necessary measures to prohibit and prevent" anyone on their territory from acquiring biological weapons. The collapse of the BWC Protocol negotiations in 2001 left the Convention without a clear direction for future efforts, a political vacuum that has been only partially filled by annual intersessional meetings.

Some countries have continued to press for a resumption of the protocol negotiations. As recently as late 2007, Iran, Pakistan, India, and Russia advocated resuming the talks, and the new U.S. administration may come under renewed international pressure in early 2009 to return to the negotiating table.

The Commission believes that the U.S. decision in 2001 to withdraw from the BWC Protocol negotiations was fundamentally sound and that the next administration should reject any efforts to restart them. History has shown that it is extraordinarily difficult to verify compliance with the BWC because virtually all biological materials, equipment, and facilities are dual-use. This verification problem has been compounded by the spread of advanced biotechnology around the world. The well-intentioned effort by the United States during the 1995–2001 protocol negotiations to promote confidence-building "transparency" was undone both by the unrealistic view of European and other allies that compliance with the BWC could be verified by an international organization and by the determination of Iran, Russia, and others to exploit the protocol to undermine international nonproliferation efforts and the convention itself.

But U.S. policy on biological weapons cannot rest solely on opposition to the BWC Protocol. It is essential that the United States lead the international community and promote a new approach for strengthening national implementation of the BWC. To signal the political importance that the United States attaches to preventing biological weapons proliferation and terrorism, the new administration should consider sending a senior-level official to address the Seventh BWC Review Conference in 2011.

During the two years leading up to the Seventh Review Conference, the United States should work with its allies and other parties to develop new initiatives aimed at achieving universal adherence to the BWC and promoting effective national implementation, especially with respect to the prevention of bioterrorism. The United States should also seek broad political support for an expanded intersessional work program that focuses on (1) building the capacities of BWC member states in key areas of bioterrorism prevention such as laboratory security, disease surveillance (including new diagnostic laboratories), and the oversight of research in the life sciences with a high potential for misuse for hostile purposes and (2) improving the practical training of experts from BWC member states in technical aspects of biosafety, biosecurity, and disease surveillance.

Finally, the United States should support an appropriate increase in the size and stature of the BWC Implementation Support Unit, currently a small staff based at the United Nations Office in Geneva, so that it can function as an effective facilitator and coordinator for an expanded set of BWC activities and initiatives.

Nuclear Proliferation and Terrorism

> Every senior leader, when you're asked what keeps you awake at night, it's the thought of a terrorist ending up with a weapon of mass destruction, especially nuclear.
>
> —Secretary of Defense Robert Gates

On October 28, 2008, Dr. Mohamed ElBaradei, Director General of the International Atomic Energy Agency (IAEA), stood at the rostrum of the United Nations General Assembly and warned the world about nuclear terror.

"The possibility of terrorists obtaining nuclear or other radioactive material remains a grave threat," said Dr. ElBaradei. A soft-spoken man, he let the power of his message make his case loudly and unmistakably—and it produced major news stories around the world. "The number of incidents reported to the Agency involving the theft or loss of nuclear or radioactive material is disturbingly high . . . ," he said. "Equally troubling is the fact that much of this material is not subsequently recovered. Sometimes material is found which had not been reported missing."

We live in a time of increasing nuclear peril. The number of states armed with nuclear weapons or seeking to acquire them is increasing. Terrorist organizations are intent on acquiring nuclear weapons or the material, technology, and expertise needed to build them. Trafficking in nuclear technology is a serious, persistent, and multidimensional problem. The worldwide expansion of nuclear power increases the danger of proliferation.

The challenges for the United States and the world remain clear. Today, anyone with access to the Internet can easily obtain designs for building a nuclear bomb, but the hardest part for those bent on nuclear terror has always been acquiring the weapons-grade uranium or plutonium required to make the bomb. Our crucial task is to secure that material before the terrorists can steal it or buy it on the black market. And we must stop and reverse the proliferation of nuclear weapons while we can.

Since the beginning of the nuclear age, the United States has made halting but steady progress toward establishing universal norms for the possession and use of nuclear weapons and toward securing nuclear materials and technology. U.S. strategies include building international regimes based on the Nuclear Nonproliferation Treaty (NPT) that came into force in 1970 and on the system of international safeguards that support its implementation. Those include counterproliferation initiatives undertaken to strengthen the nuclear security regime and cooperative programs between the United States and partner countries intended to strengthen the international response to nuclear security threats.

The United States, as a preeminent nuclear power, has an obligation to lead the world in advancing these efforts. Few other nations have the ability to exemplify best practices for the rest of the world. Few other nations can marshal the resources, expertise, and talent necessary to extend long-term bilateral and multilateral help on nuclear security issues. Our efforts must adapt to meet the rapidly evolving nuclear security challenges we confront today. After examining several tiers of U.S. efforts, the Commission offers the following findings and recommendations.

The Nonproliferation Regime

The Nuclear Nonproliferation Treaty (NPT) has been ratified by 188 nations. It established an international norm against the proliferation of nuclear weapons and an elaborate system of nuclear safeguards to monitor compliance. The NPT defines a *nuclear-weapon state* as any country that manufactured and exploded a nuclear weapon prior to January 1, 1967. This definition limits the number of "official" nuclear-weapon states to five: the United States, Russia, China, France, and the United Kingdom. At the heart of the NPT is a bargain: in return for a pledge by the non-nuclear-weapon states to forswear nuclear weapons in perpetuity, the five declared nuclear-weapon states agree to provide assistance for peaceful uses of nuclear technology and negotiate in good faith on effective measures relating to nuclear disarmament.

To demonstrate compliance with their NPT obligations, the non-nuclear-weapon states must negotiate a safeguards agreement with the International Atomic Energy Agency that permits inspections of civilian nuclear plants in order to detect the diversion of nuclear material from those plants to make nuclear bombs.

The revelation during the 1990s that Iraq and North Korea were violating their NPT obligations led the IAEA to adopt a system of strengthened safeguards in 1997. States were urged to conclude an Additional Protocol with the IAEA that greatly expanded and strengthened its monitoring rights. As of October 2008, 118 states have signed the Additional Protocol and 88 have ratified it.

Today, however, the nonproliferation regime faces major challenges. The nuclear programs of Iran and North Korea pose the most urgent and immediate threat. But the growing nuclear arsenals of India, Pakistan, and China raise serious concerns that the international community must address. The recently concluded U.S.–India Civil Nuclear Cooperation Agreement may significantly affect Asian security, and the next President will have to manage the actions that states may take in response to the agreement. The President should begin by conducting a comprehensive, all-source assessment of the agreement's impact on nuclear weapons programs in the region.

The IAEA is constrained in serving as the world's nuclear watchdog because its staff is aging and its budget has increased little over the past decade. The IAEA has been forced to rely on extrabudgetary contributions from member countries, including the United States. Because of this, the IAEA now faces uncertainties about its long-term ability to perform its fundamental mission—detecting the illicit diversion of nuclear materials and discovering clandestine activities associated with weapons programs.

Perhaps the most important challenge facing the IAEA is the expected expansion of civil nuclear programs throughout the world. New nuclear facilities will have to be carefully monitored to ensure that no nation uses peaceful activities as a cover for a secret nuclear weapons program or for diverting weapons-usable material to a weapons program. Such monitoring will increase the strain on the IAEA's already limited resources. As a first step, the United States and the IAEA should ensure that civilian nuclear facilities are designed and built with safeguards in mind.

Among the other tests facing the IAEA is the inherent difficulty of reliably detecting dangerous illicit nuclear activities in a timely fashion. Some of these difficulties—such as detecting military diversions from nuclear fuel cycle activities—are not likely to be remedied no matter how much the IAEA's resources are increased. In the past 20 years, while the amount of safeguarded nuclear material usable for weapons (highly enriched uranium and separated plutonium) has increased by a factor of 6 to 10, the budget for safeguards has not kept pace and there are actually fewer inspections per safeguarded facility than before.

In addition to limited resources, the IAEA lacks clear authority to secure nuclear material and install near-real-time surveillance at the sites it inspects, or to conduct the "wide-area surveillance" needed to monitor activities under the Additional Protocol. Dysfunctional and nontransparent national accounting practices and national procedures for inventorying nuclear materials further limit the IAEA's effectiveness, especially when coupled with the agency's increasing inability to meet its "timely detection" goals.

More fundamentally, no review has been conducted recently to determine whether the IAEA needs to update definitions—such as how much material is needed to make a bomb and how much time is required to divert this material and to convert it into bombs—that are critical to the IAEA's fulfilling its mission. Finally, two structural factors have significantly undermined the IAEA's ability to act credibly against noncompliant states. First, consensus is typically sought within the IAEA Board of Governors and the UN Security Council prior to any compliance-related actions. Second, there are no automatic, default penalties for states that cannot be found to be in full compliance with their safeguards or other NPT obligations.

While the NPT and the IAEA are at the heart of the nonproliferation regime, it is important to note that they are bolstered by national export controls that help states impede the transit of technologies that could contribute to nuclear weapons programs across their borders, and groups of countries such as the Zangger Committee and the Nuclear Suppliers Group that set international export control standards.

RECOMMENDATION 3: The United States should work internationally toward strengthening the nonproliferation regime, reaffirming the vision of a world free of nuclear weapons by (1) imposing a range of penalties for NPT violations and withdrawal from the NPT that shift the burden of proof to the state under review for noncompliance; (2) ensuring access to nuclear fuel, at market prices to the extent possible, for non-nuclear states that agree not to develop sensitive fuel cycle capabilities and are in full compliance with international obligations; (3) strengthening the International Atomic Energy Agency, to include identifying the limitations to its safeguarding capabilities, and providing the agency with the resources and authorities needed to meet its current and expanding mandate; (4) promoting the further development and effective implementation of counterproliferation initiatives such as the Proliferation Security Initiative and the Global Initiative to Combat Nuclear Terrorism; (5) orchestrating consensus that there will be no new states, including Iran and North Korea, possessing uranium enrichment or plutonium-reprocessing capability; (6) working in concert with others to do everything possible to promote and maintain a moratorium on nuclear testing; (7) working toward a global agreement on the definition of "appropriate" and "effective" nuclear security and accounting systems as legally obligated under United Nations Security Council Resolution 1540; and (8) discouraging, to the extent possible, the use of financial incentives in the promotion of civil nuclear power.

The Commission believes there are a number of specific actions that the United States should undertake to implement this recommendation.

ACTION: The United States should lead efforts to establish, as a principle of international law, penalties for states that commit serious, sustained violations of the NPT or withdraw from the treaty.

Any state that commits serious and sustained violations of its IAEA safeguards commitments or withdraws from the NPT should be required to forfeit all benefits gained from membership in the regime. The burden of proof should be on that state to prove that it is in compliance with its treaty obligations. This principle could be established either by agreement among the NPT's member states or, if that is not achievable, by a UN Security Council resolution adopted under Article VII of the UN Charter.

Such a resolution should require any state declaring its intention to withdraw from the NPT to be automatically subject to intrusive measures. These should include inspections to determine whether the state is in violation of its safeguards commitments. During this process, the state would be obligated to demonstrate its compliance with its obligations.

A country discovered—either through the intrusive measures following its declaration that it intends to withdraw from the treaty or through other means—to be in noncompliance with its safeguards obligations would be subject to stringent additional monitoring measures to determine the extent of the noncompliance. These additional measures would include (1) broad mandatory inspections; (2) access without delay to persons and original documents, with the right to record interviews and copy documents; and (3) expanded access to information. A noncompliant state would forfeit the right to further nuclear assistance. Finally, all nuclear materials, technology, and equipment a state received while a party to the NPT would be removed from that country as a condition of withdrawal from the treaty.

ACTION: The United States should lead an international effort to establish a nuclear fuel bank.

An international fuel bank would guarantee countries a supply of nuclear reactor fuel. It would also provide complying countries with storage for spent fuel; these countries, in turn, would commit not to exercise any right to establish enrichment and reprocessing facilities. Progress has been made in creating a fuel bank through the IAEA, but the IAEA Board of Governors has taken no action to address the difficult questions of how the fuel bank will be administered and the conditions for its use. Meanwhile, Russia has taken initial steps to establish itself as a regional supplier of nuclear fuel.

The idea of a nuclear fuel bank has found widespread support—its backers include President George W. Bush and IAEA Director General ElBaradei, who endorsed the idea in his October 2008 UN address: "The ideal scenario, in my opinion, would be to start with a nuclear fuel bank under IAEA auspices." By then, U.S. Energy Secretary Samuel W. Bodman had already transferred $50 million to the

IAEA for this purpose, saying, "The United States fully endorses the establishment of an IAEA fuel bank . . ."

The United States should also work to build international support for the negotiation of a treaty halting the production of fissile materials for military purposes. This would be part of an overall effort to show that Washington is moving on all fronts to strengthen the nonproliferation regime. Since, for more than a decade, the international community has been unable to conclude a Fissile Material Cut-Off Treaty, alternative approaches should be explored. A possible start could be a joint declaration by the five NPT-designated nuclear-weapon states to halt their production of fissile material for weapons.

ACTION: The United States should lead an international effort to update and improve IAEA capabilities.

The most urgent element of such an effort should be to make sure the International Atomic Energy Agency has the resources and authorities needed to meet its current and expanding mandate. The UN High-Level Panel on Threats, Challenges, and Change described the IAEA aptly: "As an institutionalized embodiment of the Treaty on the Nonproliferation of Nuclear Weapons and of considerable long-term success in preventing widespread proliferation of nuclear weapons, the International Atomic Energy Agency . . . stands out as an extraordinary bargain."

The United States should work with the IAEA Director General to secure the resources (funding, personnel, safeguard technologies, etc.) needed to meet an increasing IAEA safeguards workload. This could include establishing a safeguards "user fee," whereby countries with inspected facilities would be assessed a fee to help defer the costs.

The United States and other interested parties should take additional actions to strengthen the IAEA and improve its management. They should routinely (at least every two years) assess whether the IAEA can meet its own inspection goals; whether those goals afford "timely warning" of an ability to account for a bomb's worth of nuclear material, as required by U.S. law; and what corrective actions, if any, might help the IAEA to achieve its inspection goals. This assessment should also clarify those instances in which achieving the goals is not possible.

The United States must continue to push for universal adherence to the IAEA Additional Protocol, which provides the IAEA with additional rights to monitor civilian nuclear programs. According to the IAEA, there are now 439 nuclear power reactors in 30 countries—and 36 more plants are under construction. The U.S. government should also work to make adherence to the Additional Protocol a precondition of civil nuclear assistance under the provisions of UN Security Council Resolution (UNSCR) 1540, the rules of the Nuclear Supplier Group, and the laws of the United States.

The IAEA currently is hampered by the lack of near-real-time surveillance equipment at a number of sites where nuclear fuel rods are located and where such equipment must be installed so that the agency can establish the inspection continuity of the fresh and spent fuel rods. In addition, to promote much-needed transparency at suspect sites—and to help deter transfers of nuclear fuel and nuclear weapons technology—the IAEA member states should consider maintaining a registry of all foreign visitors at safeguarded sites. This registry should be made available to other IAEA members upon request.

To enhance the effectiveness of its safeguards program, the agency should establish a complete country-by-country inventory of nuclear materials that could be used to make nuclear bombs. The information should be shared, as appropriate, with individual IAEA member states and the public to ensure that it can be used effectively in developing the plan for IAEA safeguards. The IAEA should update the database regularly. Current IAEA databases are incomplete, and the agency's confidentiality rules make it difficult to construct a comprehensive country-by-country inventory.

The United States should accelerate the Department of Energy–led efforts to build a global database of nuclear material. To the extent possible, the United States should give the IAEA access to this data, thereby enhancing the agency's ability to carry out its mission.

The United States should also work with other IAEA members to agree that only IAEA inspectors from nuclear-weapon states (who already have access to sensitive weapons-related knowledge) should be authorized to look for indicators that weapons work is taking place at an inspected nuclear facility. Such a requirement would enhance the ability of inspectors to detect possible illegal activity at inspection sites, while minimizing the risk of spreading sensitive information.

In addition to the international efforts discussed above, the United States should improve its domestic nonproliferation efforts and set a positive example for other nations to follow. The U.S. government should (1) declare a date certain for ending the civilian use and export of highly enriched uranium (HEU) and declare a moratorium on commercial reprocessing; (2) implement Title V of the Nuclear Nonproliferation Act of 1978, which requires energy assessments for developing states; (3) secure civilian nuclear facilities in the United States that store or handle nuclear weapons–usable materials to the same standards used for securing military facilities; and (4) accelerate efforts, such as the Next Generation Safeguards Initiative of the Department of Energy (DOE), to develop advanced safeguards techniques and capabilities that will improve the global application of safeguards.

ACTION: The United States should expand counterproliferation initiatives and improve their implementation.

The counterproliferation initiatives developed by the United States and other like-minded nations complement the NPT in combating the spread of nuclear weapons. Through diplomacy, the United States must reinforce the conviction that nuclear proliferation and terrorism are concerns not of a few states but of all members of the international community.

The Global Initiative to Combat Nuclear Terrorism (GICNT) is a multilateral initiative that was announced by the United States and Russia in 2006 and now includes 75 members. Under the initiative, the United States works with Russia and other nations to promote a global sense of urgency and commitment to securing nuclear materials, developing a security culture in states where nuclear materials are stored, and preventing nuclear materials and technology from falling into terrorists' hands. These goals are to be pursued through regular joint threat briefings, nuclear terrorism exercises, and nuclear security reviews. The U.S. government should also work to enhance GICNT in key areas, such as (1) eliminating the civilian storage and use of HEU, (2) securing the weapons-usable material of participating states in the shortest possible time frame, (3) aiding participating nations in carrying out the obligations contained in UNSCR 1540, and (4) building international capacity in critical areas, such as nuclear forensics.

The United States should intensify its use of UNSCR 1540, a 2004 resolution that established binding obligations on all UN member states to take and enforce measures against WMD proliferation, to help countries develop the laws and regulations they need to criminalize proliferation, to improve physical protection and safeguards at nuclear facilities, to strengthen export controls, to improve cooperation on interdiction, and to tighten border security. The United States should also use UNSCR 1540 to work with states to develop a robust security culture focused on reducing the risk of theft or diversion of nuclear materials or technology. In particular, it should urge the adoption of "best practices" and national legislation.

The United States should also seek to strengthen the Proliferation Security Initiative (PSI), a global effort aimed at stopping the trafficking of WMD, their delivery systems, and related material. The initiative can be further improved by increasing the number of participants, enhancing efforts to interdict shipments of WMD (as well as their delivery systems and related materials), and heightening efforts to disrupt black market networks and the financing of proliferation. More importantly, the United States should also work with other states to extend the international laws that prohibit piracy, hijacking, and slavery to cover all transfers of WMD, delivery systems, and related materials in international waters and airspace.

Moreover, the United States should seek to establish as a binding requirement of international law the provision that all transfers of items on the Nuclear Suppliers Group dual-use and trigger lists must be reported in advance to the IAEA or to another international authority. Washington should assist in developing a system to process and analyze the information gathered. Any item transferred in violation of this requirement would be considered an illegal shipment—subject to seizure while in transit and to dismantlement, destruction, or return should it reach its destination. Such a requirement could be established pursuant to a UN Security Council resolution adopted under Article VII of the UN Charter.

Finally, the United States should strengthen and broaden efforts to detect and disrupt proliferation financing. Improved cooperation between the International Financial Action Task Force and countries participating in the PSI is a step in the right direction. The United States should continue to encourage other states to adopt legislation that strengthens national and international measures to combat the financing of proliferation and terrorist networks.

ACTION: The United States should orchestrate an international consensus to block additional countries from obtaining enrichment and reprocessing capabilities.

The Commission believes that one of the principal means of halting nuclear proliferation is to prevent the spread of uranium enrichment and plutonium reprocessing technologies and facilities to additional countries. It is important that the United States work to orchestrate an international consensus to block additional countries from obtaining these capabilities. The international nuclear fuel bank discussed above would be a significant step toward gaining this consensus, because it would ensure that nations without these capabilities have a reliable supply of nuclear fuel at market prices.

Many variations on the idea that no new nations should acquire enrichment and reprocessing capabilities have already been put forward. The Bush administration, for example, has proposed that the 45 members of the Nuclear Suppliers Group—the nations of the world with the most advanced nuclear technologies—refuse to sell them to any state that does not already possess full-scale, functioning reprocessing and enrichment capabilities. This proposal would effectively cap the number of states with such capabilities at current levels. Although some states have regarded this proposal as discriminatory, others, such as the United Arab Emirates, have agreed to forgo fuel cycle activities in exchange for assistance in developing civil nuclear power. Dr. ElBaradei has also weighed in, proposing that any new production-scale enrichment or reprocessing facility be under multinational control.

Both of these proposals have merit, but neither has been fully embraced by NPT non-nuclear-weapon states. Additional efforts are needed to find the right set of incentives and disincentives to gain widespread adherence.

ACTION: The United States should work with others to promote and maintain a moratorium on nuclear testing.

It is essential that current moratoria on nuclear testing, observed independently by each of the five nuclear-weapon states under the NPT, be maintained. The next President may wish to undertake diplomatic efforts to formalize such a commitment among the NPT nuclear-weapon states and should encourage non-NPT nuclear-weapon states to adopt moratoria of their own.

The Commission recognizes that the issue of a Comprehensive Nuclear Test Ban Treaty (CTBT) is likely to be reconsidered by the next administration. In 1999, the Senate decided not to provide its consent to ratification of the CTBT. The 51 senators who opposed the treaty had a variety of concerns, including (1) the potential need for the United States to resume nuclear testing under certain circumstances in order to maintain the safety or reliability of the U.S. nuclear stockpile, (2) the fact that the treaty's zero nuclear yield threshold cannot be verified, and (3) whether other parties to the treaty were in compliance with its provisions. The 48 senators who supported it argued that it would make an important contribution to strengthening the international norm against proliferation and could impede states that are considering the modernization or procurement of nuclear arsenals. They also argued that the Department of Energy's "stockpile stewardship" program would help to ensure the long-term viability of the nuclear stockpile. And they maintained that an assurance of 100 percent verifiability of the provision on zero nuclear yield was not a realistic objective.

The Commission supports the review currently being conducted by the bipartisan Congressional Commission on the Strategic Posture of the United States. That review includes consideration of the long-term reliability, safety, and effectiveness of the U.S. nuclear arsenal. The review also covers the effectiveness of the international monitoring system that is designed to identify and locate underground nuclear tests in order to evaluate the potential reconsideration of the CTBT. Out of deference to the Commission on the Strategic Posture, we have not taken a position on the CTBT in this report.

ACTION: The United States should work to gain international agreement on specific, stringent standards for securing nuclear materials.

States have a principal obligation under UNSCR 1540 to adopt and enforce "effective" measures to establish domestic control of nuclear, chemical, and biological weapons and their means of delivery. States also must establish "appropriate" controls over the related materials.

Because the resolution does not define "effective" or "appropriate" measures for nuclear security and accounting systems, there is a need to establish standards for precisely what UNSCR 1540 requires states to do. These definitions must be formulated at the highest levels to ensure that internationally agreed-on standards will be implemented by all nations. Undersecured nuclear material and facilities pose a threat not just to the host nations but to all nations. A baseline approach to establishing what measures are effective and appropriate for nuclear security and accounting standards is the best way to safeguard the world from nuclear tragedy.

The Commission recognizes the urgent need to establish global nuclear security standards to which all states can adhere. We believe that the Convention on the Physical Protection of Nuclear Material and the IAEA's Information Circular (INFCIRC) 225, *The Physical Protection of Nuclear Material,* are the building blocks for obtaining an international consensus on measures that are needed to ensure adequate nuclear security and protection. But tighter standards need to be defined. The goal of the United States should be to ensure that international standards for securing nuclear materials are as stringent as those currently defined for U.S. military facilities. It is important that ongoing negotiations to amend INFCIRC 225 seek the highest standards possible.

The Convention on the Physical Protection of Nuclear Material establishes measures on the prevention, detection, and punishment of offenses relating to nuclear material. The Commission recognizes the positive steps taken in July 2005 when the convention was amended to bind parties to protect nuclear facilities and material in peaceful domestic use, storage, and transport. Nevertheless, the amended convention does not define specific standards for a physical protection "regime." It will not enter into force until two-thirds of state parties have ratified it, an event that is unlikely to occur until well into the future.

ACTION: The United States should discourage, to the extent possible, the use of financial incentives in the promotion of civil nuclear power.

The spread of nuclear technology and nuclear material heightens concern that non-nuclear-weapon states might decide to develop nuclear weapons, building on their civilian nuclear industry. It also increases the possibility that terrorists might be able to steal—or buy from an insider—the materials or technical knowledge needed to construct a nuclear weapon. We should discourage, to the extent possible, the subsidizing of nuclear energy in ways that would cause states to choose it over other energy sources, without fully accounting for this risk.

Cooperative Nuclear Security Programs

The breakup of the Soviet Union in 1991 led to international concerns that Soviet nuclear weapons and nuclear material deployed in Belarus, Kazakhstan, Ukraine, and Russia would no longer be under the control of a strong central government. In response, the United States led a coalition of nations to persuade Belarus, Kazakhstan, and Ukraine to become parties to the NPT as non-nuclear-weapon states.

Around the same time, Congress passed the Nunn-Lugar Amendment, which established assistance programs in the former Soviet Union (FSU) to ensure the safe and secure dismantlement and transportation of nuclear weapons and the secure storage and consolidation of dangerous nuclear materials. The amendment authorized $400 million for cooperative threat reduction (CTR) programs, and appropriations have remained relatively stable over the past 17 years. These programs helped return Soviet nuclear warheads from Kazakhstan, Ukraine, and Belarus to Russia for dismantlement; led to the dismantlement and disposal of strategic missiles in Russia and other former Soviet states; and greatly improved security at Russian warhead storage facilities. Other CTR accomplishments included securing nuclear weapons and materials at vulnerable sites and enhancing the security of nuclear weapons and materials in transit.

The United States has also worked with Russia on a number of efforts to secure, reduce, and eliminate nuclear materials in Russia and to stem the illicit flow of technologies and expertise from Russia (and other FSU states) to terrorists and covert weapons programs. The Material Protection, Control, and Accounting (MPC&A) program, implemented by the Department of Energy in 1997, provides security upgrades for nuclear materials at hundreds of facilities in the FSU, including improved security systems, strict control and accounting systems for materials, and security training for Russian nuclear specialists. In 2003, Congress passed legislation requiring the Department of

Energy to complete its work by 2013, so that Russia would assume sole responsibility for sustaining security upgrades after that time. Secretary Bodman told the Commission in September 2008 that the United States and Russia are on track to meet the deadline.

The two countries have also worked to reduce the amount of material—highly enriched uranium and weapons-grade plutonium—that might be stolen and used as fuel in illicit nuclear weapons. The Department of Energy is working with its Russian counterpart to "blend down," or process into a less-enriched form, 500 metric tons of Russia's HEU, which is then shipped to the United States for use as reactor fuel. So far, this partnership has blended down almost 350 metric tons of HEU.

At the same time, Washington and Moscow have also taken steps to (1) dispose of at least 68 metric tons of U.S. and Russian weapons-grade plutonium by converting it into fuel for commercial reactors; (2) shut down Russia's three remaining plutonium-producing reactors, two of which have now been closed; (3) secure Russia's borders to prevent the illicit trafficking of nuclear materials; and (4) ensure that thousands of former weapons scientists, technicians, and engineers throughout the former Soviet Union are engaged in civilian pursuits, to prevent the flow of this expertise to countries of proliferation concern and to terrorist organizations. (The pace and scope of the DOE programs were the subject of a 2001 report titled *A Report Card on the Department of Energy's Nonproliferation Programs with Russia,* which laid out specific criteria and objectives for the programs. That study, widely known as the "Baker-Cutler Report," is discussed in detail in an appendix below.)

After the terrorist attacks of September 11, 2001, growing concerns about nuclear and radiological terrorism spurred increased cooperative efforts to secure fissile materials and combat nuclear smuggling worldwide. One outcome was the Bratislava Nuclear Security Initiative, signed by Presidents George W. Bush and Vladimir Putin in 2005, which expanded and accelerated security upgrades at nuclear sites in Russia and led to a plan for Moscow to take charge of security at its own nuclear facilities. A senior U.S.-Russia group, co-chaired by the U.S. Secretary of Energy and the Director of the Russian Ministry of Atomic Energy, oversees this work and provides progress reports every six months to the U.S. and Russian Presidents.

Increasingly, threat reduction programs are being pursued internationally, not only bilaterally with Russia. The DOE's Second Line of

Defense program seeks to prevent illicit trafficking in nuclear and radiological materials by installing radiation detectors at international land borders, seaports, and airports. Another program, the Global Threat Reduction Initiative, is a worldwide effort to reduce and protect vulnerable nuclear and radiological materials located at civilian sites; it also seeks to convert civilian research reactors worldwide from the use of WMD-usable fuel to that which can be used only in reactors. In the past several years, programs to engage nuclear scientists in civilian pursuits have been expanded to areas outside the former Soviet Union. Additionally, the Department of Homeland Security's Container Security Initiative (CSI), which now operates at 58 ports around the world, is designed to prevent dangerous nuclear materials and technologies from entering the United States. This program scans high-risk cargo before it is loaded on U.S.-bound container ships. CSI has been criticized for its reliance on shipper-provided information to determine which containers are "high-risk"; the program is supplemented by the additional scanning of containers once they arrive in U.S. ports.

RECOMMENDATION 4: The new President should undertake a comprehensive review of cooperative nuclear security programs, and should develop a global strategy that accounts for the worldwide expansion of the threat and the restructuring of our relationship with Russia from that of donor and recipient to a cooperative partnership.

When cooperative nuclear security programs started well over 15 years ago, they focused on "loose nukes" and undersecured nuclear materials in the former Soviet Union. More work remains in securing Russia's nuclear arsenal, which is spread over its 11 time zones. As former Senator Sam Nunn suggested in 2004, "We should offer to help Russia consolidate their nuclear weapons in a few areas, and then guard the heck out of them."

But cooperative nuclear security programs have evolved to address global threats as well. Terrorists seeking nuclear material will look wherever that material may be poorly secured—in Russia or elsewhere. There are currently well over 100 nuclear research reactors around the world that use HEU for fuel, and many of them lack adequate security. The November 2007 break-in by armed intruders at the Pelindaba nuclear research facility in South Africa illustrates the international challenge.

Even as nuclear security programs have expanded into important new areas, no strategic plan has been formulated to ensure maximum effectiveness and coordination across different government agencies. A new strategy is needed that takes into account developments since September 11, 2001, including the fundamental changes in Russia's economy and in U.S. relations with Russia. Equally important, the strategy should establish a basis for strengthening the international consensus on working cooperatively to address nuclear proliferation and terrorism.

The strategic review should examine every U.S. government program and activity, then recommend new, strengthened, or restructured programs where warranted; programs that are less effective should be eliminated or reduced. The review should identify where existing programs have helped stem the flow of potentially dangerous materials and technology, as well as gaps in coverage. Finally, the review should assess prospects for cooperative nuclear threat reduction activities in specific countries where concerns or opportunities may exist, such as Pakistan, India, North Korea, and China.

Washington should continue to work with Moscow to fulfill the goals of current nuclear security programs in Russia and should extend such programs to all vulnerable facilities. The Commission is concerned that Russia is not paying attention to developing an effective nuclear security culture at all Russian facilities where nuclear material is stored. The United States should propose to Russia an expansion of nuclear security commitments that would secure nuclear materials at all Russian facilities, including those storing nuclear weapons.

The United States should also press Russia to accelerate the blenddown of HEU from dismantled nuclear weapons and explore ways to expand its commitment beyond the 500 metric tons already agreed on. Moreover, the process of converting civilian Russian research reactors from using HEU to using low-enriched uranium (LEU) should be intensified.

The Commission supports the efforts by the United States and Russia to close Russia's plutonium-producing reactors and calls on both countries to finalize an agreement on disposing of plutonium in excess of defense requirements.

Finally, the Commission recommends that efforts to engage former nuclear weapons scientists in peaceful research ventures in Russia and the former Soviet republics continue and be guided by newly articulated priorities, such as focusing on nuclear institutes that are struggling financially and could be vulnerable to recruitment efforts by terrorist cells or proliferant states. The next administration should also assess the potential of these programs to work not only with nuclear weapons scientists and engineers, but with individuals at nuclear facilities who may have access to nuclear material. Although Russia's economic revival has helped mute some concerns regarding Russia's nuclear institutes, the fact remains that not all of these have benefited from this revival and some require our continued attention.

Russia no longer wishes to be seen as a recipient of U.S. or international largesse. Moscow can now afford to allocate more resources to cooperative security programs, to develop long-term plans, and to fund those plans. Whenever possible, the two countries should work to move nuclear security programs in Russia to a cost-sharing basis, a process that is already under way for some programs. Also, when possible, the United States should work with Russia as a partner to advance the objectives of threat reduction worldwide. Many U.S. threat reduction programs involving Russia are currently being implemented as partnerships. For example, the Global Threat Reduction Initiative includes trilateral programs—involving the United States, Russia, and the IAEA—to convert research reactors worldwide from HEU to LEU and repatriate the fuel back to Russia.

At the same time, U.S. cooperation with Russia should not be a prerequisite for international efforts to strengthen nuclear security. The United States should continue to work with international partners through existing vehicles to strengthen their ability to counter nuclear proliferation and combat nuclear terrorism.

The next administration must also think creatively about how to maximize the contributions of agencies other than the Departments of Defense, Energy, and State to promote cooperative nuclear security objectives. Such steps should include greater utilization of Department of Homeland Security and intelligence community assets. Also, greater coordination between the Departments of Energy and Homeland Security to improve radiation scanning devices at U.S. and international borders—and an acceleration of Homeland Security efforts to build a global nuclear detection network—would enhance the ability of the United States to track nuclear materials and prevent their movement across borders.

Country-Specific Challenges: Iran and North Korea

The Nuclear Nonproliferation Treaty is facing the prospect of an unraveling that could be its permanent undoing. Iran and North Korea have pursued nuclear weapons–related programs that the world cannot permit to succeed.

Iran's apparent efforts to acquire a nuclear weapons capability in defiance of its NPT obligations and UN Security Council resolutions and the uncertainty over whether North Korea will ultimately eliminate its nuclear weapons program constitute threats to international peace and security. Failure to resolve these crises could lead some countries to revisit their earlier decisions to renounce nuclear weapons, potentially leading to a cascade of new nuclear-weapon states. Such a wave of nuclear proliferation would seriously jeopardize the current world order, creating profound new risks and increasing instability.

Iran maintains that it does not want to acquire nuclear weapons and is merely pursuing "peaceful" nuclear activities as allowed under the NPT. Although the National Intelligence Estimate on Iran issued in November 2007 came to the controversial conclusion that Iran had ended its nuclear weapons design and weaponization work in the fall of 2003, it made clear that Iran had engaged in such weaponization work until then and continues to develop a range of technical capabilities, including a civilian uranium enrichment program, that could be used to produce nuclear weapons. If Iran should test a nuclear device or declare it possesses a nuclear weapon, or if additional evidence should come to light that conclusively revealed that Iran was making a nuclear weapon, it would be the third time since 1991 that an NPT member evaded international nuclear inspectors, using the cover of peaceful nuclear activities to either obtain, or come close to obtaining, a nuclear weapon.

If Iran should acquire a nuclear weapon in violation of its pledges without suffering severe penalties, other countries might view it as a model to follow—leading to a "cascade of proliferation," as a UN panel has warned. Several other countries, including Egypt, Algeria, Turkey, Brazil, Argentina, Saudi Arabia, Libya, South Korea, and Taiwan, have, to varying degrees and at different times, expressed interest in acquiring nuclear weapons and are now planning on expanding their peaceful nuclear energy programs.

The Commission decided that because of the dynamic international environment, it would not address the precise tactics that should be employed by the next administration to achieve the strategic objective of stopping the nuclear weapons programs of Iran and North Korea. Developing those tactical initiatives will clearly be one of its urgent priorities.

But on the central finding, the Commission was unanimous in concluding that the nuclear aspirations of Iran and North Korea pose immediate and urgent threats to the Nuclear Nonproliferation Treaty. Successful nuclear programs in both countries could trigger a cascade of proliferation and lead to the unraveling of the NPT.

Iran

For almost a decade, the United States has been concerned that Iran is pursuing a nuclear weapons program through clandestine activities as well as under the guise of peaceful enrichment for civilian nuclear power. In 2002, a London-based Iranian opposition group—the National Council of Resistance of Iran—added to such concerns by disclosing details about a secret heavy-water production plant at Arak and an underground enrichment facility at Natanz. Later that year, the United States denounced Iranian violations of the NPT and IAEA Safeguards agreement, accusing Iran of across-the-board pursuit of weapons of mass destruction.

Three years later, the IAEA Board of Governors expressed an "absence of confidence that Iran's nuclear program is exclusively for peaceful purposes." In early 2006, the board voted to refer Iran as a possible NPT violator to the UN Security Council; in December 2006, the UN Security Council ordered Iran to suspend its enrichment effort and adopted the first of three resolutions imposing sanctions to punish Iran for continued defiance of the Security Council order. Tehran insists that its enrichment program is intended only to provide fuel for nuclear power reactors essential for meeting the nation's peaceful energy needs.

As the United States was leading the effort in the UN Security Council to end Iran's enrichment efforts, the European Union (EU) established a dual-track approach, supporting UN sanctions against Iran while also offering Iran economic incentives to end its enrichment activities. The United States has not engaged in direct negotiation with Tehran, but has worked closely with the EU regarding its incentives effort. Britain, China, France, Germany, Russia, and the United States have held out the possibility of a package of political and economic benefits if Tehran suspends its enrichment of uranium. To date, these efforts to find a diplomatic solution have failed.

Most recently, on September 29, 2008, IAEA Director General ElBaradei told his agency's board of governors that Iran's continued enrichment activities are "still a cause for concern for the international community in the absence of full clarity about Iran's past and present nuclear program."

Just how much time does the world have to seek this "full clarity" and decide what to do? Experts such as David Albright, of the Institute for Science and International Security, have underscored that the timeline for Iran's acquisition of sufficient HEU to build a nuclear bomb is ominously short—it ranges from only six months to two years.

North Korea

Serious concerns over North Korea's efforts to possess nuclear weapons have played a major role in U.S. foreign policy for more than 15 years. In 1985, North Korea obtained a nuclear reactor from the Soviet Union and signed the Treaty on the Nonproliferation of Nuclear Weapons. Seven years later the International Atomic Energy Agency and North Korea finally reached agreement on a safeguards agreement (required of all NPT non-nuclear-weapon states). As a result of inspections in late 1992, the IAEA identified significant discrepancies in North Korea's declaration and demanded that "special inspections" be conducted at the Yongbyon nuclear complex. In response, Pyongyang threatened to withdraw from the NPT, prompting the United States to intervene to negotiate a resolution to the crisis. In 1994, the United States and North Korea signed the Agreed Framework under which Pyongyang agreed to a denuclearized Korean peninsula in return for political and economic concessions, including the construction of two light-water nuclear power reactors.

In 2002, after having frozen North Korea's existing plutonium-based nuclear program, the Agreed Framework completely unraveled after the United States confronted North Korean officials with information that their country was conducting a clandestine uranium-based nuclear weapons program in violation of the agreement. In an effort to resolve the crisis, a Six-Party Talks forum was formed involving China, Japan, North Korea, Russia, South Korea, and the United States. Despite a September 2005 declaration of agreement to denuclearize the Korean peninsula, this Six-Party effort failed to prevent North Korea from testing a nuclear weapon in October 2006—and declaring itself a nuclear-weapons state. Nonetheless, renewed diplomatic efforts, including direct talks between the United States and North Korea, led to the Six-Party "Initial Actions" agreement with Pyongyang in February 2007 on an overall road map for denuclearization.

The implementation of this agreement has been stop-and-go. But in mid-October 2008, some progress was made on the verification issue; the United States reciprocated by removing North Korea from its state sponsors of terrorism list. Future discussion will focus on the completeness of North Korea's declaration and the conclusion of a verification protocol.

> **RECOMMENDATION 5:** As a top priority, the next administration must stop the Iranian and North Korean nuclear weapons programs. In the case of Iran, this requires the permanent cessation of all of Iran's nuclear weapons–related efforts. In the case of North Korea, this requires the complete abandonment and dismantlement of all nuclear weapons and existing nuclear programs. If, as appears likely, the next administration seeks to stop these programs through direct diplomatic engagement with the Iranian and North Korean governments, it must do so from a position of strength, emphasizing both the benefits to them of abandoning their nuclear weapons programs and the enormous costs of failing to do so. Such engagement must be backed by the credible threat of direct action in the event that diplomacy fails.

In 2004, the UN High-Level Panel on Threats, Challenges, and Change issued a blunt warning: "We are approaching a point at which the erosion of the non-proliferation regime could become irreversible and result in a cascade of proliferation." In the past four years Iran and North Korea have made progress in their nuclear programs, and today the situation is even more urgent. We cannot, through global inaction, allow that cascade of proliferation. It could doom populations the world over.

Pakistan

The Intersection of Nuclear Weapons and Terrorism

> As I left government, the one piece of intelligence I heard that most frightened me was that al Qaeda was rebuilding a safe haven in the FATA.
>
> —A former senior counterterrorism official

Pakistan is an ally, but there is a grave danger it could also be an unwitting source of a terrorist attack on the United States—possibly using weapons of mass destruction. The Commission urges the next administration and Congress to pay particular attention to Pakistan, as it is the geographic crossroads for terrorism and weapons of mass destruction. Indeed, the border provinces of Pakistan today are a safe haven, if not the safe haven, for al Qaeda.

Al Qaeda's Afghan safe haven was critical to its ability to plan and implement its attacks of September 11, 2001. Even then, Pakistan had a role as a transit country for some of the hijackers. But now it has become a key safe haven for al Qaeda, according to the most senior U.S. intelligence official. In February 2008, Mike McConnell, the Director of National Intelligence, testified to the House Intelligence Committee: "The FATA [Federally Administered Tribal Areas] serves as a staging area for al Qaeda's attacks in support of the Taliban in Afghanistan as well as a location for training new terrorist operatives for attacks in Pakistan, the Middle East, Africa, Europe, and the United States." A year previously, his office had published a National Intelligence Estimate asserting that al Qaeda "has protected or regenerated key elements of its Homeland attack capability, including: a safe haven in the Pakistan Federally Administered Tribal Areas (FATA)." The National Intelligence Estimate added that "al Qaeda will continue to try to acquire and employ chemical, biological, radiological, or nuclear

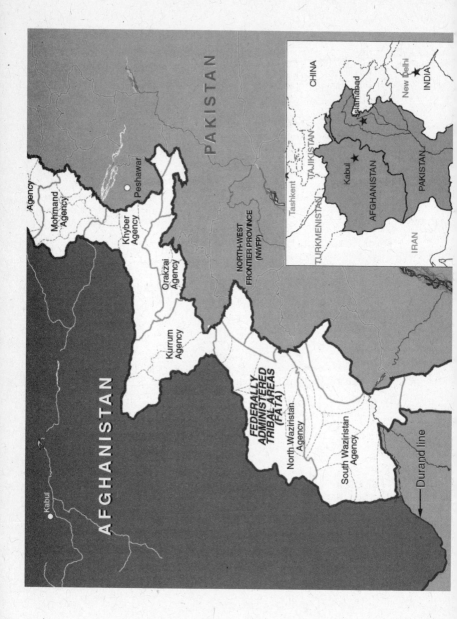

material in attacks and would not hesitate to use them if it develops what it deems is sufficient capability." Another senior intelligence official responsible for dealing with terrorism recently affirmed that al Qaeda has strengthened its ties with Pakistani militants in the past year, replenished its mid-level lieutenants, enjoys in the FATA many of the benefits it enjoyed in Afghanistan before September 11, and remains the most serious terrorist threat to the United States.

Indeed, a 2007 *Foreign Policy Magazine* poll of 117 nongovernmental terrorism experts found that 74 percent consider Pakistan the country most likely to transfer nuclear technology to terrorists in the next three to five years. Pakistan is a nuclear-weapon country; it gained this status through the illicit work of a nationalist Islamic scientist, A. Q. Khan. He was the father of Pakistan's "Islamic bomb" and the purveyor of sensitive nuclear technology across the Middle East and Asia—to Libya, North Korea, and perhaps other countries. His network of business associates spanned the globe and is only now being fully brought to justice. There may be other Pakistani scientists who have been, or would be, willing to work with other countries or with terrorists to help them acquire nuclear weapons.

According to open source estimates, today Pakistan has about 85 nuclear weapons, which are under the complete control of the Pakistani military. Though most U.S. and Pakistani officials assert that these weapons and their components are safe from inside or outside theft, the risk that radical Islamists—al Qaeda or Taliban—may gain access to nuclear material is real. Should the Pakistani government become weaker, and the Pakistani nuclear arsenal grow, that risk will increase. With each new facility, military or civilian, comes added security concerns.

The reality is that Pakistan is steadily adding to its nuclear weapons stockpile, which remains its chief deterrent against Indian attack. In October 2008, on the heels of the U.S.-India civil nuclear agreement, China agreed to build two nuclear power plants in Pakistan. This deal—especially if it does not contain mechanisms to prevent nuclear material from being transferred from the new civilian plants to military facilities—signals a nascent nuclear arms race in Asia.

The risk of a WMD attack being planned and executed from Pakistan's northwest frontier area is growing, as that area continues to function as a safe haven for al Qaeda.

RECOMMENDATION 6: The next President and Congress should implement a comprehensive policy toward Pakistan that works with Pakistan and other countries to (1) eliminate terrorist safe havens through military, economic, and diplomatic means; (2) secure nuclear and biological materials in Pakistan; (3) counter and defeat extremist ideology; and (4) constrain a nascent nuclear arms race in Asia.

The President and Congress should develop and implement a comprehensive policy involving all elements of national power—military, economic, and diplomatic—to eliminate terrorist safe havens in Pakistan. This policy should also be implemented with regard to Afghanistan, India, China, and Russia.

ACTION: The United States should continue to support Pakistan's efforts to eliminate al Qaeda's safe haven in the Federally Administered Tribal Areas (FATA) and the North-West Frontier Province (NWFP), through increased joint military and intelligence operations. The United States should also support Pakistan's efforts to work with tribal leaders and to strengthen the Frontier Corps and local police.

The United States should continue to provide Pakistan direct military support in the hunt to capture or kill al Qaeda and Taliban terrorist leaders. The United States, with other countries, should also provide funding and training to the Pakistani military, as well as to the Frontier Corps and other local and provincial security forces. Where possible, any operations should be executed by Pakistani forces; the U.S. military footprint in Pakistan should remain minimal.

Allowing the Pakistani armed forces to lead the fight, supported by the United States, other North Atlantic Treaty Organization members, and other friendly countries, avoids further arousing Pakistani nationalism and anti-Americanism. Minimizing direct U.S. involvement lessens the opportunity for nationalist outcry and may allow a more rational assessment of the situation. The Pakistani government, military, and people need to understand that their interests are also at stake—an unfortunate reality driven home by the assassination of Benazir Bhutto and by the September 2008 attack against the Islamabad Marriott. Al Qaeda and radical militants pose a threat to Pakistan's democratic government, institutions, and people. Ultimately, the only way for a democratic Pakistan to truly take on al Qaeda and other terrorists is for all elements of the society to recognize them as a threat not just to the United States or Europe but also to Pakistan itself.

ACTION: The new U.S. policy toward Pakistan should include economic assistance that helps Pakistan improve the services it provides to its people and create greater opportunities for education and commerce, especially in the FATA.

The focus of U.S. policy should be to help Pakistan achieve political and economic stability. Current U.S. assistance to Pakistan reflects the decision to make tactical, near-term military and security concerns a priority over long-term efforts to bolster Pakistan's democracy and its prospects for economic development. Over the past six years, the United States supported Pakistan with a mix of military, security, economic, and social aid, totaling $12 billion. Of that total, $8.9 billion (74 percent) was devoted to security and military assistance, and only $3.1 billion (26 percent) went to social and economic programs.

Yet festering economic and social ills in Pakistan have created a hospitable environment for radicalization, and the trends indicate that the challenge is growing. Pakistan's population is projected to double to nearly 300 million people by 2050, making it the world's fifth most populous country. Over the next decade, food, water, and energy are likely to become scarcer. The UN Development Program's Human Development Report of 2005 gave Pakistan the lowest score for its education index of any country outside of Africa. Pakistan's overall literacy rate hovers between 40 and 50 percent. For women, the literacy rate is below 30 percent—and for women in the FATA, it is only 3 percent. Because teachers are poorly trained, Pakistanis are turning away from public education to attend private schools and madrassas, most of which offer religious instruction rather than preparing youth to enter professions or trades.

The Commission supports the type of assistance proposed in legislation sponsored by Senators Joseph Biden and Richard Lugar in July

2008—S. 3263, the Enhanced Partnership with Pakistan Act of 2008. This bill was envisioned as a "democratic dividend" to the democratically elected post-Musharraf government, and if passed it will provide a down payment on democracy and security. In a statement accompanying the legislation, the lawmakers asserted: "The purpose and intent of this legislation is to help transform the relationship between the U.S. and Pakistan from a transactional, tactically-driven set of short-term exercises in crisis-management, into a deeper, broader, long-term strategic engagement." The bill authorizes $1.5 billion annually for five years for nonmilitary assistance to Pakistan—more than triple the current funding.

Any U.S. assistance should be designed to reach local leaders and entities as directly as possible, in order to strengthen civil society. Emphasis should be placed on developing infrastructure in border provinces: hospitals, roads, power plants, and schools (with teachers who are well trained). Such investments in physical infrastructure are easy to measure and monitor. They also provide opportunities to enhance cross-border trade, promote tourist corridors, and encourage specific businesses, such as selling electricity.

Such opportunities result in both economic development and confidence building between Pakistan and its neighbors. In addition, they symbolically demonstrate the commitment of the United States to the people of Pakistan. The cumulative effect of this new strategy for U.S. development and economic assistance would be to help the Pakistani people, foster their government's ability to provide services and effective governance at all levels and in all parts of the country, and, ultimately, provide the antidote to terrorist safe havens and a bulwark against radicalization.

If the United States does not change the emphasis of its assistance, Senators Biden and Lugar said in their joint statement, "there is little likelihood of drying up popular tolerance for anti-U.S. terrorist groups, or persuading any Pakistani regime to devote the political capital necessary to deny such groups sanctuary and covert material support."

ACTION: The new U.S. strategy toward Pakistan should involve the use of all elements of national power—including those of so-called soft power, such as public diplomacy, strategic communications, and development assistance—to counter violent extremist anti-Americanism, create a universal culture of revulsion against the use of WMD, and lower the demand for WMD by terrorists.

The U.S. objective should be not only to address the underlying social, economic, and educational conditions that give rise to violent extremism and terrorism but also to use all means to counter the messages of terrorists. By addressing the basic needs of the Pakistani people and letting them know that the United States is not solely interested in supporting Pakistan's military, this new approach will demonstrate U.S. commitment to the people of Pakistan. If accompanied by effective public diplomacy, it can help foster a climate in which the democratic Pakistani government will be able to work with the United States in a stronger partnership, one based on mutual concern for the Pakistani people. The potential benefits of U.S. assistance were illustrated recently, albeit briefly, in the aftermath of the October 2005 earthquake in Pakistan, when the United States provided over half a billion dollars in relief. The terrorists tried to compete, but the U.S. assistance was so large-scale and visible that Pakistanis began giving out small toy Chinook helicopters—the main purveyors of the food, blankets, and medicine. In return, the United States received a great deal of Pakistani goodwill.

Shifting the U.S. message and support from emphasizing the military to stressing development assistance and support to the institutions of Pakistani government will demonstrate that the U.S.-Pakistan relationship is founded on more than the war on terror. If U.S. public diplomacy succeeds in countering radical Islamist anti-American ideas in the mosques and coffee shops in Pakistan, then there is a chance that the United States can erode tacit or explicit support for terrorists who espouse mass violence, including the use of weapons of mass destruction.

We emphasize that it is not enough for leaders at the highest levels to understand the importance of tools of soft power and decide to use them. They must also develop the organic capability to deploy those tools where and when needed around the world—including, in the first instance, in Pakistan. In the section below titled "Government Organization and Culture," we outline what such an organic capability entails and recommend the steps necessary to reorganize the civilian foreign policy agencies in much the same way as the military and the intelligence communities have been restructured.

ACTION: The President must make securing biological and nuclear materials and weapons in Pakistan a priority. Congress should ensure that sufficient funding is authorized and appropriated for this purpose, and other countries such as Russia and China should be enlisted to contribute to this effort.

Providing assistance to Pakistan to ensure that its nuclear facilities are secure from theft or any diversion of materials, weapons, or expertise is a vital security interest for the United States and for the international community. Therefore, the new U.S. strategy for Pakistan must emphasize working with the Pakistani military and with Pakistani and other foreign intelligence services to make certain that all threats to Pakistan's facilities can be minimized, anticipated, and countered.

Moreover, Pakistan has biological research laboratories that possess stocks of dangerous pathogens, some of which may not be adequately secured. The United States is currently funding efforts to improve physical security and access control at such facilities. This support should continue until Pakistan has sufficiently reduced the potential danger of theft or accidents.

Several Russian officials with whom the Commission met in Moscow in September 2008 indicated that they supported working with the United States to help the Pakistani government maintain and improve the security of its nuclear arsenal. The executive director of a Russian nongovernmental organization focused on nonproliferation asserted that the most urgent need for bilateral cooperation directed at other countries concerned Pakistan, not Iran. This expert added that working with Pakistan "could be the leading subject of nonproliferation cooperation" between the United States and Russia.

Such an international effort could have the added benefit of supporting the creation of a consensus among countries that do not now recognize the risks posed by WMD proliferation and terrorism. It could focus their attention on biological and nuclear security, proliferation networks, and international terrorism.

ACTION: The United States should work with Pakistan, India, China, Russia, and other countries to constrain the nascent arms race in Asia and to reduce tension and promote greater stability in that region. As part of this effort, the United States should encourage cross-border activities, such as people-to-people exchanges, transportation, trade, and economic investment.

The President must engage India and Afghanistan to foster a common understanding that Pakistani stability and progress are in their own interest and in the best interests of South Asia generally. In particular, Pakistan's deeply adversarial relationship with India so consumes strategic thinking in Pakistan that little attention is paid to such concerns as counterterrorism and nonproliferation. Easing tension between the two nations should give Pakistan the space to recognize its stake in addressing these issues.

The United States should work with Russia to engage Pakistan, India, and China in a regional approach to nuclear security and counterproliferation. Priority should be assigned to precluding the use of nuclear weapons during a future crisis, further securing nuclear materials, limiting the expansion and modernization of nuclear forces, continuing the current nuclear testing moratorium, precluding onward proliferation to the Middle East, and limiting the deployment of short-range nuclear delivery systems. At the same time, U.S.-Indian cooperation in the civilian nuclear power industry must not be allowed to become the catalyst of a nuclear arms race in Asia. U.S. policy must seek to counter the destabilizing aspects of Chinese, Indian, and Pakistani nuclear modernization and address the root causes of insecurity that fuel proliferation.

An existential fear of India is the main preoccupation of the Pakistani military. Pakistan's nuclear modernization is driven both by India's conventional modernization and by the prospect of India's nuclear expansion. India's nuclear and conventional modernization, in turn, is driven by fears of China and Pakistan.

Pakistan believes that it is surrounded by security threats—and U.S. cooperation with India in defense and strategic technology sharing has exacerbated this perception. Multiple sources of instability in South Asia dilute the ability of the Pakistani government to focus on any one specific security issue, thereby allowing all of them to worsen. If Pakistani leaders are preoccupied with threats from India's nuclear forces and the insurgency in Kashmir, then their cooperation with the United States on issues of concern to the United States will be limited.

Findings and Recommendations

The United States should build confidence in Pakistan through its Afghanistan policy. That policy should aim to stabilize Afghanistan by ridding it of the Taliban and allied extremists, build stability in border provinces such as Baluchistan, and assure Pakistan that U.S. policy toward Afghanistan will not result in collaboration between India and Afghanistan at Pakistan's expense. Al Qaeda recognizes the value of exploiting Pakistan's concern with both India and Afghanistan.

If the Pakistani government could be reassured about its own external security, it could focus more attention on internal elements such as governance, civic services, and the need to counter radicalization. To achieve this goal, the United States must display greater transparency in its diplomatic exchanges with Pakistan, including its clarification of the U.S.–India civil nuclear deal. And it must also persuade Islamabad that U.S. assistance to India is not a direct threat to Pakistan's strategic security.

Finally, the United States should discreetly encourage a return to a back-channel dialogue between India and Pakistan, supported by confidence-building measures. As discussed in the next section, working with Russia could be an effective way to pursue such measures. This effort should be part of a broader regional strategy to help ensure that disputes and instability in Kashmir and Pakistan–Afghanistan border provinces do not become flashpoints that destabilize regional security.

○ ○ ○

It is possible for the situation in Pakistan to take a more positive turn. After the bombing of the Marriott Hotel in Islamabad, Pakistani President Asif Ali Zardari declared that the war on terrorism "is our war." Parliamentarians are being briefed on the terrorist threats and on Pakistani military operations in the border regions. Tribal leaders are organizing against foreign al Qaeda elements in the FATA and NWFP. Suicide bombing has been declared illegitimate by Muslim scholars of all major schools of thought in Pakistan. Relations between Afghanistan and Pakistan appear to be improving, and negotiations may help separate the committed terrorists from those who have legitimate grievances against their governments.

Nevertheless, there is no graver threat to U.S. national security than a WMD in the hands of terrorists. Trends in South Asia, if left unchecked, will increase the odds that al Qaeda will successfully develop and use a nuclear device or biological weapon against the United States or its allies. The reality behind the 9/11 Commission's comment that "it is hard to overstate the importance of Pakistan in the struggle against Islamist terrorism" is obvious. The difference today is that the situation is urgent.

Russia and the United States

There can be no coherent, effective security strategy to reduce nuclear dangers that does not take into account Russia—its strengths, weaknesses, aims, and ambitions.

—Senator Sam Nunn

Since 1991, the United States and Russia have had a shared commitment to reducing nuclear weapons in the arsenals of both nations. The Strategic Arms Reduction Treaty (START), signed by the United States and the Soviet Union in July 1991, was the first strategic arms control treaty to actually call for a reduction in the number of nuclear warheads deployed by the two parties.

One of the most difficult issues facing the new administration will be relations with Russia. It is safe to say that over the past decade the post-Soviet promise of a democratic Russia has not materialized, and concerns about how Russia is exercising its interests in eastern Europe and the states of the former Soviet Union are increasing.

As Washington and Moscow struggle to resolve their foreign policy differences, preventing WMD proliferation and terrorism remains a critical shared interest. Both countries acknowledged this common aim as recently as April 2008, when they agreed to the U.S.–Russia Strategic Framework Declaration. Despite serious differences on many foreign policy issues, the two sides agreed on a Joint Framework for their relationship that emphasizes strategic arms, nuclear nonproliferation, and the fight against global terrorism. It is remarkable that during a tense period, the United States and Russia could come together to chart a new relationship. Their Joint Framework provides a basis for moving forward on many of the recommendations of this Commission.

Biological Cooperative Threat Reduction

At its peak, the illicit biological weapons program of the Soviet Union employed an estimated 50,000 scientists and technicians. After the Soviet breakup in 1991, the United States launched a major effort to prevent this dangerous expertise from migrating to rogue states and terrorist organizations. The United States sought to find civilian employment for former Soviet bioweapons scientists. In recent years, however, the United States has reluctantly cut back its biological cooperative threat reduction (CTR) activities in Russia because of Moscow's bureaucratic and political obstacles. Increasingly, the Russian government has viewed biological CTR programs with disinterest and even suspicion, arguing that its growing economic strength obviates the need for continued foreign assistance. Yet despite these assertions, Russia's former bioweapons scientists and inadequately secured collections of highly dangerous pathogens remain a global proliferation concern.

Nuclear Security Initiatives

The 2005 Bratislava Nuclear Security Initiative contained a comprehensive joint action plan for cooperation on security upgrades that accelerated security upgrades, performed in Russia by U.S. officials, of nuclear weapons and material sites. It also included specific benchmarks and timelines for upgrades of the nuclear sites controlled by the Federal Atomic Energy Agency (Rosatom) and the Ministry of Defense. Since the signing of the Bratislava Initiative, additional sites have been added to the Material Protection, Control and Accounting Program; work there is to be completed by the end of fiscal year 2010. More needs to be done, however; in particular, both the focus on Russian civil nuclear facilities and the pace at which they are secured must be increased. The Bratislava Initiative is a successful model for bolstering efforts to cover additional nuclear sites in Russia, and the United States may seek to follow it in addressing the remaining military and civilian sites.

While security upgrades for sensitive Russian nuclear facilities have expanded and accelerated under the Bratislava Initiative, senior Russian officials have not paid sufficient attention to their need to sustain these upgrades after the U.S. programs come to a close. The National Defense Authorization Act of 2003 mandates that a sustainable material security system be transferred to the exclusive support and management of the Russian Federation no later than January 1, 2013. The current Joint Sustainability Plan identifies the requirements for Rosatom to sustain the improvements made possible by U.S.-provided assistance, and the two sides are working on an implementation plan. But to date, the Russian government has not shared with Washington its plans to fund sustainment of the security upgrades. More needs to be done to secure a Russian commitment to increase funding for these efforts.

Strategic Nuclear Arms

When the Soviet Union broke apart in December 1991, some of the nuclear weapons covered by START were located in Ukraine, Kazakhstan, and Belarus. After a series of U.S. initiatives and offers, these nations agreed to eliminate all of their nuclear weapons during the seven-year reduction period outlined in START I and to join the Nonproliferation Treaty as non-nuclear-weapons states. The treaty limits land-based intercontinental ballistic missiles (ICBMs), submarine-launched ballistic missiles (SLBMs), and heavy bombers on the territories of the parties and imposes a complex verification regime.

All the nuclear warheads located in Kazakhstan, Ukraine, and Belarus were returned to Russia for elimination. The United States and Russia completed the reductions in their forces by the designated date in December 2001. START will expire in December 2009 unless the parties agree to extend it. The United States and Russia have indicated that although they do not support extension of START as a whole, they are interested in extending some of the treaty's verification provisions. According to the treaty, the parties must begin discussions about the future of the treaty one year prior to its expiration. Senior-level discussions between the United States and Russia began more than a year ago, but basic questions, such as which START transparency provisions should be extended, have not been resolved.

The United States and Russia committed to further reductions in their strategic nuclear arms in the Strategic Offensive Reductions Treaty. This pact, referred to as the Moscow Treaty, was signed in May 2002 and entered into force in June 2003. It has two basic requirements: (1) that the United States and Russia reduce their strategic nuclear warheads to between 1,700 and 2,200 warheads by the treaty's expiration date of December 31, 2012, and (2) that both parties meet at least twice annually in a Bilateral Implementation Commission established by the treaty to discuss its implementation. The May 2008 Report on the Implementation of the Moscow Treaty states that the number of U.S. operationally deployed nuclear warheads was 2,871 as of December 31, 2007. Although the U.S. estimate of the number of Russian warheads is classified, it is known that Russia is also making considerable progress toward the Moscow Treaty limit. Neither party expects to have any difficulty meeting the treaty limit. The treaty contains no monitoring provisions.

The recent political environment has led to fears of a resurgent Cold War relationship between the United States and Russia. The upcoming expiration of START and, not long after, of the Moscow Treaty will end the formal U.S.–Russian arms reduction and transparency regime unless the two nations reach agreement on further strategic reduction measures. Despite the political tensions, they have been discussing possible ways of resolving the limits and transparency issues. But significant differences remain.

The Commission believes that the shared interests of the United States and Russia on crucial security matters such as further reductions of nuclear arsenals must transcend the tensions of the past several years.

RECOMMENDATION 7: The next U.S. administration should work with the Russian government on initiatives to jointly reduce the danger of the use of nuclear and biological weapons, including by (1) extending some of the essential verification and monitoring provisions of the Strategic Arms Reduction Treaty that are scheduled to expire in 2009; (2) advancing cooperation programs such as the Global Initiative to Combat Nuclear Terrorism, United Nations Security Council Resolution 1540, and the Proliferation Security Initiative; (3) sustaining security upgrades at sensitive sites in Russia and elsewhere, while finding common ground on further reductions in stockpiles of excess highly enriched uranium; (4) jointly encouraging China, Pakistan, and India to announce a moratorium on the further production of nuclear fissile materials for nuclear weapons and to reduce existing nuclear military deployments and stockpiles; and (5) offering assistance to other nations, such as Pakistan and India, in achieving nuclear confidence-building measures similar to those that the United States and the USSR followed for most of the Cold War.

Findings and Recommendations

The Commission believes these recommendations can best be achieved by undertaking a number of specific actions.

ACTION: The United States must work with Russia to reinvigorate cooperative biological threat reduction programs in Russia.

The next administration should launch a high-level political initiative that impresses on Russian leaders the need for continued international cooperation on biological security and nonproliferation issues. In addition, in view of the changes in Russia since the CTR program began in the early 1990s, the Department of State should lead an interagency effort in 2009 to rethink and restructure the CTR program to align it with the circumstances and challenges in Russia today.

ACTION: The United States must work with Russia to sustain security upgrades at Russian nuclear sites.

The United States should continue to press hard for a Russian commitment to adequate and transparent funding for the long-term sustainability of the security measures at Russia's sensitive nuclear facilities. Plans should be accelerated, consistent with U.S. and Russian commitments and statements under the Bratislava Initiative, as well as the U.S.–Russia Strategic Framework Declaration of April 2008 and other agreements.

ACTION: The United States must work with Russia to negotiate a post-START strategic nuclear framework.

The Commission believes it imperative that we continue to reduce the size of the U.S. and Russian nuclear stockpiles in a structured and transparent manner. Consequently, we believe that the next administration should engage with Russia at the earliest possible date to negotiate additional reductions in both countries' strategic stockpiles and to agree on transparency measures that can be in place by the end of 2009, when START expires. Such an agreement would send an important signal to the rest of the world regarding U.S. and Russian commitments to negotiate in good faith on effective measures relating to nuclear disarmament. Setting additional benchmarks for further reductions would serve as a natural reinforcement to continue this important strategic partnership in fighting terrorism and the proliferation of weapons of mass destruction.

ACTION: The United States should work with Russia and others to promote India–Pakistan confidence-building measures.

India and Pakistan have agreed to confidence-building measures that cover peripheral issues such as providing an annual listing of some of their nuclear facilities and establishing hotlines between their military directors general and between their diplomats. To date, because of a fundamental lack of trust between the two governments, these measures have not addressed core security issues or questions of nuclear command and control issues due to a fundamental lack of trust between their governments. If the United States and Russia were to lead a multi-national effort, drawing on their own experiences during the Cold War, this might help India and Pakistan to begin implementing confidence building measures to ameliorate expected destabilizing aspects of their future nuclear force modernization.

Additional measures that could be taken under the leadership of the United States and Russia to promote nuclear stability in South Asia are discussed in the preceding section of this report.

Government Organization and Culture

The massive departments and agencies that prevailed in the great struggles of the twentieth century must work together in new ways, so that all the instruments of national power can be combined. Congress needs dramatic change as well to strengthen oversight and focus accountability.

—The 9/11 Commission Report

The White House

Members of Congress and experts inside and outside of government have noted that no single person is in charge of and accountable for preventing WMD proliferation and terrorism, with insight into all the committees and interagency working groups focused on these issues. Indeed, the current Deputy National Security Advisor for Counterterrorism told the Commission that he devotes only about 15 percent of his time exclusively to WMD terrorism and that the Senior Director for Counterproliferation does the same. (He subsequently explained that certain Homeland Security Council officials spend 100 percent of their time on matters related exclusively to WMD terrorism.)

Reacting to these concerns, Congress passed the Implementing Recommendations of the 9/11 Commission Act of 2007 (Public Law 110-53)—establishing the Office of the United States Coordinator for the Prevention of Weapons of Mass Destruction Proliferation and Terrorism. The Coordinator would serve as the principal advisor to the President on all matters relating to the prevention of WMD proliferation and terrorism. The Coordinator would also be responsible for formulating, advocating, and overseeing the execution of a comprehensive and well-coordinated U.S. policy and strategy in this area.

The Bush administration initially opposed creating the position of the WMD Coordinator, arguing in a Statement of Administration Policy that such a post was unnecessary "given extensive coordination and synchronization mechanisms that now exist within the executive branch." The White House also raised constitutional concerns, suggesting that Congress cannot direct the President to establish a Senate-confirmed position within the National Security Council (the office in which the Coordinator would logically reside). As of this writing, the position has remained vacant for nearly 15 months. In September 2008, the administration briefed the Commission on a recently developed proposal regarding the Coordinator. Since it was so close to the presidential election, the Commission counseled the White House to discuss this proposal with the incoming administration before making a final decision on it.

Although we have come a long way since 9/11, one of the central criticisms leveled by virtually every commission and panel that studied what went wrong leading up to the attacks of 9/11 was that the U.S. government suffered from a serious lack of coordination among the various agencies whose job it is to keep us safe.

Today, the President's national security policymaking is overseen by two parallel councils: the National Security Council (NSC) and the Homeland Security Council (HSC). The artificial distinction between "national security" and "homeland security," emerged after the attacks of September 11, 2001, and resulted in the creation of the HSC to complement the NSC. Each council has its own supporting staff and coordinating mechanisms. The HSC has focused on a rapidly expanding area of policy over the past several years, but having two separate councils and staffs has caused redundancy and has also diffused accountability through multiple, often conflicting policy-coordinating mechanisms.

The number of Policy Coordinating Committees (PCCs) that deal with WMD issues has increased, accompanied by a considerable duplication of committee agendas and taskings. Information provided to the Commission by various agencies revealed nearly 200 interagency committees and working groups that address WMD, counterproliferation, and counterterrorism issues.

For example, one agency calculated that its senior officials attend

- 22 PCCs, sub-PCCs, interagency working groups, and interagency policy groups that hold weekly meetings
- 69 that hold monthly meetings

- 198 that hold meetings annually, semiannually, quarterly, bimonthly, monthly, biweekly, weekly, or on an ad hoc basis

A significant side effect of the redundant coordinating meetings is their consumption of considerable senior-level time and attention. Officials from the agencies that participate in all these meetings shared their concerns with our Commission.

"There are some issues that nobody manages," one agency official told the Commission, "and other issues that have too many managers." A number of officials from various agencies spoke of multiple meetings with a lack of sufficient coordination. According to one official, too much time at White House meetings was spent on management issues and not enough on strategic thinking. Another official said that he spends so much time going to interagency meetings that his time for actually performing his agency job was very often "crowded out."

RECOMMENDATION 8: The President should create a more efficient and effective policy coordination structure by designating a White House principal advisor for WMD proliferation and terrorism and restructuring the National Security Council and Homeland Security Council.

The Commission endorses specific actions to implement this recommendation.

ACTION: The next Congress should amend Public Law 110-53 to eliminate the requirement to establish an Office of the United States Coordinator for the Prevention of Weapons of Mass Destruction Proliferation and Terrorism, while retaining the mandate to appoint a senior presidential advisor with the responsibilities of the Coordinator.

The Commission strongly endorses the creation of a senior White House advisor whose sole responsibility is to serve as the President's advocate and overseer of the policy nexus between WMD proliferation and terrorism. The position of senior advisor could readily be placed within the National Security Council structure. Alternatively, such an advisor could be placed within the office of the Vice President or made the head of a separate White House office.

The Commission is concerned that the provision of the 2007 act requiring that this position be Senate-confirmed could raise issues of authority and conflicting guidance within the Executive Office of the President. Senate-confirmed officials are normally accountable to Congress and can be called to testify, but the NSC staff members advise the President and do not appear before Congress. Senate confirmation would therefore likely compel the next President to place the Coordinator outside of the NSC staff.

In short, the next President may well prefer that the senior advisor not be a Senate-confirmed position. If he does, we believe that Congress should amend the law to reflect the President's decision.

We emphasize that to be effective, this senior advisor must be seen as speaking for the President by all relevant departments and agencies, as well as the White House. He or she must have the authority to call meetings, task agencies, and resolve interagency conflicts. The advisor must also have the budgetary authority (including a direct link to the Office of Management and Budget) to assess funding levels, fix shortfalls, and adjust programs. The advisor should play the lead role in coordinating policies and operations to prevent WMD proliferation and terrorism and would be responsible for advising the President about how policy decisions across government—foreign policy, defense, trade, and so forth—would affect the mission of preventing WMD proliferation and terrorism.

Such an advisor would have enormous responsibilities and would need to exercise commensurate authority across agency lines. The advisor should not be, or be perceived as, a junior appointee. Accordingly, the Commission urges the appointment of a person of recognized distinction in the field of WMD proliferation who would enjoy the full support and confidence of the President. The senior advisor must be seen as the alter ego of the President on issues of WMD terrorism and proliferation.

The Commission believes that this senior advisor should also play a central role in promoting a strong working relationship with Congress on preventing WMD proliferation and terrorism. In particular, the advisor could help bring improved clarity to those issues about which there is a substantial difference between Congress and the executive branch.

The advisor should seek to constructively intervene on the critical issue of container port security, which has recently become contentious. Congress included in the Implementing Recommendations of the 9/11 Commission Act of 2007 a requirement that by 2012, all cargo containers must be scanned before being shipped to the United States. The Departments of Energy and Homeland Security have taken steps to scan a portion of cargo overseas, and nearly all cargo as it arrives in the United States, but they have resisted meeting the comprehensive requirement included in the law, arguing that a risk-based approach focused on the largest ports overseas is more cost-effective.

Finally, the advisor should also ensure that appropriate red team exercises are conducted across the federal government with respect to WMD terrorism prevention, preparedness, and response. Red teaming is done by designated operational and subject matter experts to discover weaknesses in a plan and to identify how it can be improved. Red team exercises, conducted in structured environments to avoid the risk of public panic, can give participants an opportunity to test procedures and to identify gaps—operational, analytic, or technical—and whatever authorities are needed prior to an actual event.

ACTION: The next President should restructure the Homeland Security Council and National Security Council by consolidating both staffs under the NSC framework. Congress should revisit the statutory creation of the Homeland Security Council and evaluate whether two separate councils are necessary.

The U.S. government must abandon the notion that "homeland" security is somehow different from "national" security, much as it has recognized that domestic intelligence, which is largely focused on the homeland, is a central element of protecting national security. Operationally, the U.S. government functions without recognizing a division between national security and homeland security, yet these seams exist in policy coordination, and indeed have been institutionalized. The creation of the Homeland Security Council was a stopgap measure to coordinate a subset of national security policies while the Department of Homeland Security was being established. Now that the Department of Homeland Security is fully operational, however, the two parallel councils create ambiguity and unnecessary redundancy, lead to multiple and conflicting policy coordination mechanisms, and dilute accountability for specific issues.

To resolve these problems, the responsibilities of the HSC staff should be transferred to the NSC staff and redundancies should be eliminated. The Homeland Security Advisor should continue to serve as the President's principal advisor for preparedness and response to natural disasters and for vertical integration of federal, state, local, tribal, and territorial authorities. The Homeland Security Advisor would also be responsible for public-private cooperation on issues such as critical infrastructure protection and for interacting with organizations such as the National Governors Association, the National League of Cities, the United States Conference of Mayors, and chambers of commerce.

Congress

The current structure of congressional oversight of national security is a relic of the Cold War. It has not evolved in response to the changing nature of the threats that the United States faces in the 21st century.

Since the dawn of the atomic age, Congress has undergone substantial reorganization only once and partial reform rarely. The Legislative Reorganization Act of 1946 restructured committee jurisdictions. In the 1970s, some incremental reforms were undertaken. And the few other reforms enacted in the 1990s were, in the view of most analysts, largely cosmetic.

Congress has pressured the executive branch to reform itself in ways that reflect the crosscutting, transnational nature of many of today's national security threats. Yet Congress has carried out only minor reforms of its own structure, instead preserving institutional stovepipes and protecting jurisdictional turf. Congressional oversight has thus been hampered by the fact that national security priorities such as the federal government's efforts to prevent weapons of mass destruction proliferation transcend the antiquated jurisdiction of any single committee.

Two recent commissions have called for fundamental changes in the national security oversight structure of Congress.

The National Commission on Terrorist Attacks Upon the United States (9/11 Commission) proposed a new, unified structure for the oversight of intelligence and counterterrorism programs, through one of two models: (1) a single committee in each chamber of Congress, with combined authorizing and appropriating authorities, or (2) a joint bicameral committee, modeled after the Joint Committee on Atomic Energy. The 9/11 Commission also proposed the creation of a single streamlined oversight structure for homeland security.

The Commission on the Intelligence Capabilities of the United States Regarding Weapons of Mass Destruction (the Silberman-Robb Commission), which focused on the intelligence community's abilities to identify, warn about, and respond to WMD proliferation and related threats, recommended "that the House and Senate intelligence committees create focused oversight subcommittees; that the Congress create an intelligence appropriations subcommittee and reduce the Intelligence Community's reliance on supplemental funding; and that the Senate intelligence committee be given the same authority over joint military intelligence programs and tactical intelligence programs that the House intelligence committee now exercises."

Congress responded to those calls for substantive change in the structure of congressional oversight by taking a few incremental steps—some of which made the legislative oversight process more cumbersome.

The Senate removed the term limits for members of the Select Committee on Intelligence, thereby allowing experienced members to continue serving (as they do on other Senate committees). The House of Representatives created a Select Intelligence Oversight Panel on the Appropriations Committee to review budget requests for intelligence activities and to align authorizations and appropriations for intelligence community activities. The panel includes members from the Appropriations Committee and the House Permanent Select Committee on Intelligence.

In response to the 9/11 Commission's recommendation to create dedicated oversight committees for the Department of Homeland Security (DHS), the House formed the Homeland Security Committee, while the Senate merely renamed its Governmental Affairs Committee—which became the Senate Homeland Security and Governmental Affairs Committee—and gave it additional jurisdiction over DHS.

But other House and Senate congressional committees still retained their jurisdiction over the agencies that had been moved into DHS. Thus, the creation of these new committees (and subcommittees) did nothing to streamline the number of congressional panels to which DHS must respond. In the House, 16 committees and 40 subcommittees now assert jurisdiction over DHS. In the Senate, 14 committees and 18 subcommittees share this responsibility.

The need for DHS to report to multiple committees and subcommittees makes it more likely that the department will receive conflicting direction from Congress, and unnecessarily increases its workload. By relying on such a splintered structure, Congress has jeopardized its ability to perform effective oversight of DHS. As Thomas Mann and Norman Ornstein have observed, "Congress' failure to oversee the DHS has been crushing."

"It was a disappointment but came as no surprise to us that the Congress did not act on the Commission's recommendations," Lee Hamilton, the former Vice Chairman of the 9/11 Commission, noted in late 2007. "It is much easier for the Congress to reform the Executive branch than it is to reform its own institutions."

That Congress has yet to adequately organize itself to cope with the nuclear age, much less the post-9/11 era, is deeply troubling and demands action. We understand that reforming and streamlining the processes of Congress is not easy; members of Congress understandably do not like to relinquish the committee or subcommittee chairmanships they worked for and waited years to obtain. We also recognize that leaders from both parties in Congress have pushed for reforms, with some successes. But the urgency of the situation requires that Congress do much more.

RECOMMENDATION 9: Congress should reform its oversight both structurally and substantively to better address intelligence, homeland security, and crosscutting 21st-century national security missions such as the prevention of weapons of mass destruction proliferation and terrorism.

We are the third bipartisan commission to urgently and unanimously recommend that the legislative branch reorganize its oversight and budgeting processes so as to most effectively work to prevent WMD terrorism. Given the threats now facing the United States, the difficulties of institutional change and jurisdictional competition are not acceptable excuses for the failure to act on these recommendations.

Congress's failure to reform itself has resulted in ineffective oversight of important national security threats and missions that transcend the jurisdiction of a single committee. These include federal efforts to assess and prevent WMD proliferation and terrorism. One consequence of Congress's failure to adapt to the evolving nature of national security threats is the outsourcing of national security oversight to external commissions like this one.

The next President should establish a greater level of trust by reaching out to Congress on intelligence issues, improving consultation with the intelligence committees, and making clear that Congress should play a vigorous role in overseeing intelligence. For its part, Congress should use its oversight to build cooperation and a shared sense of mission with the intelligence community and the President. The leaders of Congress should take responsibility, especially in their own parties, for ensuring that members do not make intelligence a political issue. This cooperative approach must be balanced by Congress's legitimate interest in checking executive branch power and protecting civil liberties.

ACTION: Congressional leadership should establish an Intelligence Subcommittee on the Appropriations Committees in both chambers of Congress with jurisdiction over the National Intelligence Program and Military Intelligence Program budgets. These subcommittees should include members drawn from committees with oversight responsibilities for programs funded by the National Intelligence Program or the Military Intelligence Program.

The creation in 2007 of a Select Intelligence Oversight Panel on the House Appropriations Committee was a positive first step toward long-overdue reform, but Congress needs to go further. Specifically, separate House and Senate Appropriations Intelligence Subcommittees should be created and given responsibility for both the National Intelligence Program and the Military Intelligence Program. The annual appropriations bill for the two types of intelligence programs would be reported by this new subcommittee and then passed to the full Appropriations Committee in both chambers, without substantive review by any other subcommittee.

In the Senate, the National Intelligence Program and the Military Intelligence Program budgets are appropriated through the Defense Appropriations Subcommittee. This arrangement poses a number of challenges. While the authorizers on the Senate Select Committee on Intelligence devote a large majority of their time to overseeing the intelligence budget, the attention of defense appropriators is divided across the greatly increased post-9/11 budgets, emergency supplementals for the conflicts in Iraq and Afghanistan, and a larger National Intelligence Program that funds sensitive and critical operations. Today, the challenges and risks of the post-9/11 world demand the full-time attention of an appropriations subcommittee.

ACTION: The Senate and House Homeland Security Committees should be empowered as the sole authorizing oversight committees for the Department of Homeland Security and all agencies under the department's jurisdiction.

While recognizing that crosscutting programs may require consultation with other committees, the Senate and House Homeland Security Committees should be empowered as the sole oversight committees for DHS and commit to producing annual authorization bills for the department's activities. Committees that traditionally have had jurisdiction over agencies that are now a part of DHS should no longer have this authority. It is in the interest of DHS, Congress, and ultimately the nation to streamline and strengthen congressional oversight.

ACTION: Congress should build capacity to conduct effective oversight of crosscutting terrorism and WMD issues by such means as creating an office on the model of the Office of Technology Assessment.

Because of current jurisdictional stovepipes, the congressional oversight structure discourages rather than fosters coordination on crosscutting issues. On nuclear terrorism, for example, the Homeland Security Committees may address homeland preparedness and response, but they may not be able to discuss potential sources of fissile material or overseas efforts to prevent nuclear weapons proliferation—because jurisdiction for those issues rests in the Foreign Relations,

Intelligence, and Armed Services Committees. The committees must do more to share information on crosscutting issues such as WMD proliferation and terrorism, and they must have experienced staff members with the appropriate expertise.

To enhance the technical and scientific expertise available to members, Congress should expand fellowship and detail opportunities from the nongovernmental sector. And to provide advice to members of Congress on technical issues, Congress should establish an office similar to the Office of Technology Assessment, which served this function for 23 years. In a recent positive development, some Intelligence Committee members and staff directors participated in training programs aimed at enhancing their oversight.

ACTION: Congress should work with the next administration to ensure that key aspects of U.S. law are followed with respect to required assessments of nuclear proliferation risks and the relative economic cost of civilian nuclear projects overseas.

A large body of domestic law has been developed over the past half-century to guide U.S. nuclear nonproliferation policy. The Atomic Energy Act of 1954, for example, requires nonproliferation assessment statements for any proposed nuclear cooperative agreement. But Congress did not hold hearings on Turkey or Saudi Arabia, nor did it conduct a review of the cooperation arrangements with Russia or India, particularly to ensure that the latter complies with the Henry J. Hyde United States–India Peaceful Atomic Energy Cooperation Act of 2006. Congress should make every effort to conduct a complete review of nuclear cooperation agreements that are presented to the legislature.

A second shortcoming in congressional oversight of nonproliferation activities is its failure to hold the executive branch accountable for laws regarding the safeguarding of peaceful nuclear programs. Under the Atomic Energy Act of 1954, the U.S. government is required to ensure that International Atomic Energy Agency inspections (of nuclear technologies or materials controlled under international agreements) are capable of providing "timely warning" of any diversions for military purposes. But the executive branch has not defined the requirements for IAEA inspections to provide "timely warning," nor has it indicated whether inspections of U.S.-origin nuclear materials meet the standard. Congress has failed to address the issue.

Finally, there has been no attempt to implement Title V of the Nuclear Nonproliferation Act of 1978, which requires the U.S. government to do general and country-specific assessments of the relative merits of nuclear and non-nuclear energy sources for meeting the energy needs of developing nations. Such comparative assessments are needed to inform decisions on U.S. support for proposed nuclear power projects in such states as Egypt, Turkey, India, and Saudi Arabia and to assist other developing states in perfecting their own energy plans.

The Intelligence Community

The intelligence community is implementing the most sweeping organizational changes since 1947 in response to the Intelligence Reform and Terrorism Prevention Act of 2004. Congress created the Office of the Director of National Intelligence (ODNI) to serve as the head of the U.S. intelligence community and to improve coordination among the 16 intelligence agencies. Although important work remains, significant progress is being made with respect to cross-organizational integration of intelligence collection and analysis. Past barriers to performing joint intelligence work are weakening and the number of collaborative efforts is increasing.

The Commission believes that praise is warranted to Congress for its efforts to push intelligence community reforms and to all of the agencies for their responses both to congressional initiatives and to the attack on 9/11. Examples of important new initiatives include the work of the National Counterterrorism Center (NCTC), the ODNI's 500 Day Plan, the revised Executive Order 12333, and the revised Attorney General Guidelines. Interviews with numerous current and former intelligence officers, as well as policymakers and nongovernmental experts, lead the Commission to believe that many of these reforms need time to settle and mature. Over the past four years, the intelligence community has had five different leaders. Creating additional organizational churn at this time is unlikely to serve the best interests of U.S. national security or to enhance the performance of the intelligence community. CIA Director Michael Hayden recently noted in public comments, "We have been pulled up by the roots to check how we are growing on about an 18 month cycle for about the last six years. . . . We're suffering reform and transformation fatigue." Under the circumstances, and recognizing that further reform might well be advisable in the future, we make no substantial recommendations relating to such changes at this time. We think it best to allow the current process of reform to continue unabated without significant added organizational change.

We note that despite the progress that has been made, small pockets of resistance to the changes brought about by the congressionally mandated reforms persist. The Commission found that some senior CIA officers continue to resent and resist the changes that shifted authority for leadership and management of the intelligence community to the DNI. A former CIA executive described the CIA's attitude as "rage toward the ODNI." While that view may represent only a subset of CIA personnel, the Commission encountered multiple examples of senior CIA officers expressing hostility and disdain toward the ODNI. The CIA Director needs to make organizational cooperation a priority.

In addition, while there have been significant improvements in integrating foreign and domestic intelligence, persistent cultural gaps remain. Some of these gaps can be attributed to the legacy of distinct missions and to the functional boundaries that previously existed between agencies of foreign intelligence and domestic law enforcement. The FBI continues to evolve from a purely law enforcement organization to a national security organization with significant responsibilities for detecting and preventing terrorism.

The creation of the FBI's National Security Branch and its WMD Directorate is certainly a step in the right direction. The recent revisions to the Attorney General Guidelines provide standards, procedures, and authorities intended to help the FBI perform more effective domestic intelligence collection and analysis. However, greater collaboration between the intelligence and law enforcement communities is needed to foster common understanding of the tools and best practices that each may adopt.

The Commission also found that considerable progress has been made with respect to improving information sharing across federal departments and agencies, as well as with state, local, and tribal governments. The creation of state information fusion centers has improved domestic information sharing. Such efforts are certainly laudable, but they must be pursued in effective coordination with other efforts such as the FBI's Joint Terrorism Task Force model. In that model, state, local, and federal law enforcement and intelligence agencies conduct joint investigations of counterterrorism cases and work to disrupt plots against the U.S. homeland.

In short, the Commission believes that the intelligence community is aggressively implementing the changes required by the Intelligence Reform and Terrorism Prevention Act of 2004. We propose no further organizational changes to the community at this time. However, the next President should direct the DNI to continue to look for ways to streamline redundant organizations, layers of management and staff, including a review of the effectiveness of the recently created National Counterproliferation Center. As discussed below, the DNI should identify challenges to current human resource strategies and propose solutions to enhance the capabilities of the current workforce.

As part of the post-9/11 reforms, two new organizations were established: the National Counterterrorism Center (NCTC) and National Counterproliferation Center (NCPC). The directors of these two organizations act as "mission managers," or senior coordinators, for all intelligence community efforts relating to terrorism and to WMD proliferation, respectively.

The NCTC coordinates both intelligence and policy implementation on counterterrorism issues throughout the executive branch. The director of this center reports to the DNI; he or she also reports directly to the President on matters of strategic operational planning. The director ensures that the operations and activities of executive branch departments and agencies are consistent with the President's priorities. The NCTC pulls together policy analysts and field operators from across the U.S. government counterterrorism community, including foreign service officers, DHS officers, FBI agents and analysts, active duty military, and personnel from the Department of Energy and other agencies. The center produces its own coordinated analyses on terrorism and publishes warnings, alerts, and advisories. The NCTC bridges the counterterrorism and counterproliferation nexus in strategic planning as well as analysis.

In contrast to the broader mission of the counterterrorism center, the role of the National Counterproliferation Center is limited to improving coordination and information sharing across the intelligence community with respect to the collection and analysis of information on WMD proliferation and related hard targets. The NCPC identifies long-term proliferation threats and requirements and develops strategies to ensure that the intelligence community is well positioned to address them. The NCPC also reaches out to elements inside and outside the U.S. government to identify new methods or technologies that can enhance the intelligence community's capability to detect and defeat future proliferation threats.

Two recent milestone events—the terrorist attacks of 9/11 and the 2002 Iraq WMD estimate that resulted in sustained criticism of the intelligence community—had a significant impact on the analytic community. But the counterterrorism (CT) and counterproliferation (CP) communities took away very different lessons from those events. Among the conclusions drawn by the CT analysts after 9/11 was that they must be far more forward-leaning in their threat assessments and must be willing to think creatively and take analytic risks. In contrast, the lessons the CP analysts drew from the 2002 Iraq WMD National Intelligence Estimate were to check and recheck every source, fully vet all information, clearly distinguish what is known from what is judged, and be extraordinarily cautious, even reticent, when preparing intelligence and presenting it to policymakers.

In an effort to apply a more uniform set of analytic standards and practices, the ODNI created the Analytic Integrity and Standards Office in 2006. As a result, sourcing standards, the use of alternative analysis, and the vetting of sources have improved. For example, all human source information used in National Intelligence Estimates must be reviewed and validated by the National Clandestine Service prior to final review and approval by the National Intelligence Board.

Effective collaboration between analysts and collectors is required. The Commission found that the relationship between analysts and collectors has improved in some areas, and that one goal of intelligence reform legislation—ensuring that analysis drives collection—is becoming a reality. The most significant progress has occurred at the national level in organizations such as the National Counterterrorism Center, where analysts and collectors from different organizations work collaboratively. Senior government officials told the Commission that the act of placing personnel from the CIA, FBI, Department of Defense, Department of Energy, and other agencies together in one office has done more to improve information sharing and collaboration than have any technological solutions. Personnel working in such an interagency setting come to understand the strengths, weaknesses, and roles of other agencies and see how the different agencies fit together as pieces of a whole. But the Commission also found that progress has been slower in individual agencies, where analyst-collector integration requires reaching across organizational barriers.

○ ○ ○

Meeting Future Needs

Half of today's analysts entered the intelligence community after 9/11. Because of attrition and hiring freezes during the 1990s, there are few midcareer analysts. Consequently, analysts are being called on to assume greater technical and managerial responsibilities earlier in their careers. In particular, the Commission found that the intelligence community's base of science and technology expertise is not sufficient to meet emerging demands in these areas.

With regard to nuclear weapons, the number of technical experts available to the intelligence community is declining because of retirements and the reduction in innovative nuclear weapons–related work at the U.S. national laboratories. Nuclear expertise remains in high demand by the intelligence community because it serves as a hedge against breakout capability and other technological surprises by state and non-state adversaries. Accordingly, such expertise should be protected as a national resource.

In the field of biotechnology, engaging experts outside of government is particularly important, because developments are fast-moving and most relevant expertise resides in academia, nongovernmental organizations, and the private sector. The Biological Sciences Expert Group, an advisory body to the National Counterproliferation Center that gives the intelligence community access to outside scientists, is an example of effective collaborative engagement with nongovernmental experts to work on high-priority issues.

In addition, the number and diversity of the potential counterterrorism and counterproliferation targets present a major challenge for collection. The main problem, a former senior CIA operations officer succinctly told the Commission, is "collecting the dots" rather than "connecting the dots."

Particularly difficult is collecting intelligence on suspect state and non-state biological weapons programs. Bioweapons programs can be hidden in seemingly legitimate scientific and industrial organizations; they can be conducted in innocuous-looking facilities; and it can be challenging to identify what is going on inside them through technical means.

Richard Danzig, a former Secretary of the Navy, has argued that traditional collection methods are not effective in this area and that a paradigm shift is needed. Danzig maintains that intelligence collection must adapt to the decentralized and transnational nature of biological risk—and he has proposed an equally decentralized approach that he calls "peripheral vision," which would take advantage of the international networks among scientists, both formal and informal.

Such networks could be valuable for acquiring information, as well as for detecting anomalous activities that might be related to state or terrorist bioweapons efforts. The Commission believes that this approach is an innovative solution to the problem of information collection and that an outreach strategy to the scientific community should be developed in order to tap into this vast reservoir of open-source information.

> **RECOMMENDATION 10:** Accelerate integration of effort among the counterproliferation, counterterrorism, and law enforcement communities to address WMD proliferation and terrorism issues; strengthen expertise in the nuclear and biological fields; prioritize pre-service and in-service training and retention of people with critical scientific, language, and foreign area skills; and ensure that the threat posed by biological weapons remains among the highest national intelligence priorities for collection and analysis.

Both within and across intelligence community agencies, the compartmentation of information remains a formidable challenge. A senior intelligence official responsible for information sharing told the Commission staff that the flow of WMD-related information in the intelligence community is still much less than it should be. Interviews with intelligence community analysts revealed a significant growth in the number of codeword compartments related to WMD proliferation and terrorism. One senior intelligence official expressed concern to Commission staff about stovepiping within the analytic communities that deal with counterproliferation, counterterrorism, and regional issues. Another senior official noted that compartmentation to preserve secrecy makes it difficult for these communities to exchange information.

> **ACTION:** The intelligence community should improve the sharing of WMD proliferation and terrorism intelligence as a top priority, and should accelerate efforts to ensure that analysts and collectors receive consistent training and guidance on handling sensitive and classified information.

If analysts and collectors working against a common target do not have access to all relevant information about the target, the mission will be less likely to succeed. To ensure that sensitive sources and methods as well as privacy and civil liberties are protected, innovative methods to manage risk must accompany greater information sharing. Adopting uniform standards for handling sensitive information and increasing trust across the intelligence community are goals that have not yet been fully achieved.

> **ACTION:** The intelligence community should expedite efforts to recruit people with critical language capabilities and cultural backgrounds. In conjunction with this effort, the intelligence community should streamline the hiring process, especially for applicants with critical language capabilities.

In order to prevent and counter efforts by terrorists to acquire WMD, it is imperative that human intelligence collection officers be able to gather information on the related activities of terrorist groups. This mission requires personnel with the necessary language skills, as well as ethnic and cultural backgrounds, to gain access to the communities where terrorist groups operate.

Since the implementation of Foreign Language Strategic Program in May 2003, the CIA has increased its overall language capability by 50 percent. The number of employees with tested capability in the agency's 10 mission-critical languages rose by just over 16 percent in fiscal year 2007 alone. However, for some of these languages the overall number of officers with proficiency is still too low.

The Commission believes that the intelligence community should continue and accelerate its efforts to hire and train individuals with critical skills and backgrounds for the counterproliferation and counterterrorism missions. To that end, the process for granting security clearances must be streamlined, while background investigations must remain thorough enough to ensure that national security is not compromised.

ACTION: The intelligence community should address its weakening science and technology base in nuclear science and biotechnology and enhance collaboration on WMD issues with specialists outside the intelligence community, including nongovernmental and foreign experts.

The use of cutting-edge science and technology is crucial in addressing WMD terrorism collection and analysis. This need is greater in the field of biology (more than two dozen types of bacteria, viruses, and other pathogens have been adopted or considered for use as biological warfare agents by states and non-state actors) than in nuclear science (nuclear weapons incorporate highly enriched uranium and plutonium as the primary types of fissile material). Furthermore, advances in genetic engineering and synthetic biology have raised the possibility of creating, respectively, modified versions of existing pathogens or entirely new pathogens. Advanced aerosolization technologies are also available from commercial sources.

ACTION: The intelligence community and law enforcement should continue to focus and prioritize collection on WMD state and non-state networks that include smuggling, criminal enterprises, suppliers, and financiers, and they should develop innovative human and technical intelligence capabilities and techniques designed specifically to meet the intelligence requirements of WMD terrorism.

The nexus of proliferation and terrorism is a top collection priority for the intelligence community, and the array of targets is massive. They include transnational terrorist and extremist groups, supplier networks, criminal organizations, front companies, financiers, smugglers, and the WMD capabilities of state and non-state actors, to name a few.

The ability to identify and counter foreign denial and deception activities is particularly critical in the area of WMD proliferation and terrorism. Therefore, maintaining and improving the intelligence community's ability to counter such efforts must be a top priority. Although the United States continues to have an intelligence advantage in some areas, this advantage will erode as foreign knowledge of U.S. systems and capabilities increases. Reversing this trend requires the development of intelligence systems that provide "unexpected, unwarned, and unconventional" collection capabilities, and these methods must be better protected from unauthorized disclosure.

ACTION: The President, in consultation with the DNI, should provide to Congress within 180 days of taking office an assessment of changes needed in existing legislation to enable the intelligence community to carry out its counterterrorism, counterproliferation, and WMD terrorism missions. In so doing, the intelligence community must keep WMD terrorism a top priority while ensuring that the broader counterterrorism and counterproliferation efforts do not suffer.

The National Security Workforce

Despite recent initiatives, the U.S. national security community still lacks the flexibility and workforce culture needed to attract, train, and retain people with the skills needed to help the government respond to global network threats such as terrorism and proliferation.

In May 2007, President Bush issued Executive Order 13434, National Security Professional Development, which focuses on building and maintaining a new generation of national security professionals. Subsequently, in November 2007, an implementation plan was published to guide the executive steering committee, chaired by the Director of the Office of Personnel Management, in recruiting, training, and retaining the necessary personnel.

RECOMMENDATION 11: The United States must build a national security workforce for the 21st century.

The Commission believes there are several specific actions that the United States should undertake to implement this recommendation.

ACTION: The U.S. government should recruit the next generation of national security experts by establishing a program of education, training, and joint duty with the goal of creating a culture of interagency collaboration, flexibility, and innovation.

The U.S. government lacks the flexibility of the private sector to accommodate individuals who are inclined to switch jobs frequently and forgo long-term stability in return for rapid professional growth and new challenges. Unless the government can offer careers that provide continuing professional and intellectual challenges, it will have difficulty attracting the best and the brightest.

The President should establish a government-wide professional education and training program for the national security officer corps, covering multiple stages of officers' careers and including curriculum on combating terrorism and WMD proliferation. To facilitate the creation of an interagency professional education program in national security, the Office of the Director of National Intelligence and the cabinet secretaries must develop a strategic plan that takes into account that, unlike the Defense Department, the intelligence community and most other national security agencies lack the manpower to assign officers to extended training programs without suffering a drop in operational capability.

ACTION: The National Security Professional Development Implementation Plan must meet its requirement to recruit, train, and retain sufficient national security professionals, including at the U.S. national laboratories.

The U.S. national laboratories have a critical need for an influx of new, highly trained personnel. The Commission's interviews with Secretary of Energy Samuel W. Bodman and other high-level officials of the Department of Energy, Sandia National Laboratories, the intelligence community, and the Department of Homeland Security all elicited concerns that the current workforce at the national laboratories is aging and will soon retire.

According to Secretary of Defense Robert Gates, "Half of our nuclear lab scientists are over 50 years old, and many of those under 50 have had limited or no involvement in the design and development of a nuclear weapon. . . . By some estimates, within the next several years, three-quarters of the workforce in nuclear engineering and at the national laboratories will reach retirement age." There are serious uncertainties about how the government will replace individuals with highly specialized skills as they retire, especially in light of the competition for these skills from the private sector. Today's scientists do not see the laboratories as innovative places to work and build challenging careers. No concerted effort has yet been made to recruit the "next generation" workforce—but without that workforce, our long-term national security is threatened.

> **ACTION:** The implementation plan must ensure incentives for distributing experience in both combating terrorism and combating WMD. The President's top national security officials should consider including assignments in more than one department and agency as a prerequisite for advancement to the National Security Council or to department or agency leadership level.

Greater opportunity for education and training is a necessary but not sufficient condition for creating an effective national security workforce for the 21st century. To foster true interagency collaboration, national security officers from across the government must have the experience of working closely with colleagues from other agencies. The Department of Defense pursues this goal through joint duty requirements, and a recent directive from the DNI mandated that intelligence officers must serve a joint tour before they are eligible for promotion to senior service. But the requirement for joint duty should begin early in an officer's career. In addition, the U.S. government should promote and fund advanced education in both nuclear science and biology, as well as joint training for crisis response, including the expeditious and effective delivery of federal capabilities to state and local governments and to foreign partners.

Global Ideological Engagement

The United States has been successful at using its defense and intelligence resources to capture or eliminate individuals involved in al Qaeda's quest for a WMD capability. But our nation has been less successful at using persuasion to deter terrorist recruitment and indoctrination of individuals who might someday use a nuclear or biological weapon against Americans or our allies.

Efforts to prevent terrorist recruitment cannot rely on the same predominantly military tools that are used to capture or kill terrorists and facilitators. Instead, the U.S. government must be more creative in developing "non-kinetic" measures to engage the enemy ideologically. U.S. counterterrorism strategy must effectively use the tools of soft power if we are to prevent WMD terrorism. Doing so will require cultural changes within the civilian foreign policy and national security agencies similar to the changes that have occurred within the military and the intelligence community.

These powers of persuasion include, at a minimum, the capability to project targeted messages about America's intentions and beliefs in support of specific foreign policy goals and to undermine the terrorists' credibility and recruiting efforts by assisting allied countries in developing greater social and economic stability at the grassroots level. To be effective in this undertaking, the U.S. foreign policy community must define its role in our efforts to stop the proliferation and use of WMD.

RECOMMENDATION 12: U.S. counterterrorism strategy must more effectively counter the ideology behind WMD terrorism. The United States should develop a more coherent and sustained strategy and capabilities for global ideological engagement to prevent future recruits, supporters, and facilitators.

The U.S. foreign policy community needs to alter its culture and organization so that it can work across agency lines to make soft power an option just as viable and effective as hard power. This change is essential; it should be a top priority of the next President's foreign policy team.

ACTION: The Secretary of State, in conjunction with the U.S. Agency for International Development and other departments, should take the lead in building an organic capability within the civilian agencies of the U.S. government for coordinating, integrating, and delivering foreign assistance, public diplomacy, and strategic communications. These efforts must be integrated under a single overarching strategy.

At present, such a coherent strategy is lacking. Like foreign assistance, programs for public diplomacy and strategic communications are dispersed throughout the U.S. government, and they are executed without coordination to ensure that they emphasize consistent messages and reinforce U.S. policy. To remedy these weaknesses, the Secretary of State should develop an integrated strategy for global ideological engagement that supports U.S. foreign assistance efforts, including a government-wide assessment of what capabilities are needed and how to create them within civilian agencies.

The Secretary should develop this strategy in close coordination with the President's senior advisor on WMD proliferation and terrorism, so that the senior advisor can consider how global ideological engagement can contribute to the overall effort to prevent WMD terrorism. The Secretary of State should then develop a process to coordinate this integrated strategy, ensuring that consistent messages accompany all public diplomacy and foreign assistance initiatives. At the same time, the strategy should be flexible enough that it can be tailored to different regions and countries. The next administration should also consider how best to reinvigorate USAID to deliver development and humanitarian assistance in an integrated fashion.

Communicating U.S. values and interests to a global audience is a major challenge in an era of instantaneous communications and 24-hour multimedia news reporting. Traditional vehicles, such as Voice of America and Radio Free Europe/Radio Liberty programming, which once reached their targeted listeners only via shortwave radio, are now available as webcasts and telecasts, in many different languages—and their English-language broadcasts have a wide global audience. But other states and non-state interests are also seeking to influence world opinion and have moved swiftly to utilize the communications tools of the 21st century. China is beaming extensive programming into Africa, in English, at a time when the U.S. government has proposed cutting the budgets for English-language broadcasting. At present, al Qaeda is using a full arsenal of media resources.

The United States must develop a comprehensive strategy for implementing this crucial facet of its public diplomacy—something that is currently lacking. The Under Secretary of State for Public Diplomacy and Public Affairs should design and implement a strategic communications plan to support global ideological engagement and buttress deterrence. The aim of this strategy should be to create a sense of revulsion against the idea of WMD terrorism, conveying the message that it is in everyone's interest to prevent groups like al Qaeda from acquiring such weapons. The President should engage foreign partners, especially in Muslim countries, and stress that al Qaeda's acquisition and use of WMD would be a catastrophe for all mankind.

In addition, the strategic communications plan should work to reframe Cold War deterrence strategy to address 21st-century threats. Public diplomacy and strategic communications can help promote awareness and cooperation internationally and in the private sector (industry and academia), especially regarding the prevention of bioterrorism and the misuse of biotechnology. The deterrence strategy should make clear to smugglers and facilitators that trafficking in WMD materials, technologies, or expertise is a redline. If they cross it, they will unite nations against them, resulting in the total disruption of their operations. Terrorist groups can be deterred if they believe that a particular weapon or tactic is likely to fail—and also if they become convinced that even if they have short-term success, the people whose support they most desire will turn vehemently against them. This should be another important tool in our efforts to halt terrorist efforts to obtain WMD.

As part of this plan, the President should expand the declaratory policy that threatens harsh retaliation against any state that assists a terrorist group in acquiring and using a WMD. This declaratory policy would mention possible retaliatory options and should be aligned with public statements and strategic communications, such as high-level discussions with foreign leaders. For the policy to be credible, however, the United States must demonstrate effective nuclear and biological attribution capabilities.

The United States should fight violent extremist ideology with the same commitment with which it contained Communist ideology. This commitment should include the application of cultural and ideological pressure at all points of the globe to counteract terrorist violence and nihilism.

The Role of the Citizen

In personal preparedness, each individual can make a huge difference. It is really an area where you can empower the individual.
> —Secretary of Homeland Security Michael Chertoff

Tom Brokaw was doing his homework in early September 2008, reviewing his old calendars and personal documents. As the former managing editor and anchor of *NBC Nightly News,* he had long estab-lished a rule that he would cover the news but not make it. But he decided to break that rule. He agreed to testify at the Commission's hearing in New York City because he wanted to provide a detailed per-sonal narrative of how events unfolded in 2001, when two of his assis-tants came in contact with a white powder that spilled out of two envelopes that had come in the mail, addressed to him. His testimony was riveting as he walked us through the weeks of wrong guesses and misdiagnoses before medical authorities realized that his two assis-tants were victims of cutaneous anthrax. Brokaw's assistants eventually recovered but his story was an example of the destructive power of anthrax when used as a weapon.

But there was something else that Brokaw did before appearing at our hearing that produced an insight every bit as valuable. It high-lighted why our Commission concluded that this section on the need to inform and empower citizens was a fitting way to end our report.

Tom Brokaw told us he wanted to see just what the U.S. govern-ment has done since 2001 to better inform citizens about attacks from this specific weapon of mass destruction:

> So I thought I would check [the] Homeland Security website
> before I came down here today. I typed in "anthrax attack." I

got a keynote address by the assistant secretary of health on the meaning of an anthrax attack, remarks by the Homeland Secretary Michael Chertoff, a testimony by a physician before the House of Representatives, testimony of an assistant secretary chief medical officer about how a prophylaxis program will be initiated early to reduce the economic impact of anthrax. I got almost no information that would be useful [to] me in that culture of chaos if I needed help to find out where I go, what it looks like, and what the next course of action should be.

A well-informed and mobilized citizenry has long been one of the United States' greatest resources. While much of this report has focused on what the U.S. government must do to prevent the use of weapons of mass destruction, it is also important to recognize the contribution that all Americans can make in preventing such an attack against our country.

Faced with a serious problem of homegrown terrorism, the United Kingdom has come to recognize the untapped power of the British people in countering radicalization. During a meeting with our Commission, a senior Scotland Yard official succinctly expressed the British law enforcement agency's conclusion: "Communities defeat terrorism."

The British government has embraced the reality that the public can represent a vast early warning network. Cooperative relationships between citizens and law enforcement are becoming a major weapon in combating terrorism and radicalization in the United Kingdom. The United States has much to learn from the British example. A concerted effort is needed to involve the American public in prevention efforts. This effort should start by developing a public education program that goes well beyond the vague admonition to report "suspicious activities." The public must be made aware of what activities are suspicious and of their responsibility to inform authorities.

The public must also be prepared for its role in responding to a potential WMD attack. Citizens must be educated about what they should expect from their government in such a crisis—and what government expects from them in the form of advance preparation and responsible action. If we show potential terrorists that we are ready—as a community and as a nation—then they are less likely to believe that their attack can achieve all of its destructive goals.

RECOMMENDATION 13: The next administration must work to openly and honestly engage the American citizen, encouraging a participatory approach to meeting the challenges of the new century.

The Commission believes there are several specific actions that the United States should undertake to implement this recommendation.

ACTION: The federal government should practice greater openness of public information so that citizens better understand the threat and the risk this threat poses to them.

Although the Commission did find relevant government-created content regarding anthrax on the website of the Centers for Disease Control and Prevention, it is clear from Brokaw's testimony that more must be done to educate the public regarding what information is available and where to find it. Of course the information should be easily accessible. In the event of an attack, quick access to information can save untold lives. The government would be well served to have ready-made messages, adaptable to the circumstances of any specific event, available for swift distribution following an attack. Such messages could be delivered by government officials; natural social networks, such as schools and churches; and the media, including the Internet.

The Department of Homeland Security's use of color-coded threat levels was well intentioned, but it has resulted in highly simplistic representation of the nation's risk. Citizens are often confused by the meaning of changes in threat levels and do not know what actions they should take in response. If such an advisory system is continued in the next administration, changes in threat levels should be accompanied by explanatory statements and by recommendations of appropriate actions.

ACTION: The next administration should, as a priority, work with a consortium of state and local governments to develop a publicly available checklist of actions each level of government should take to prevent or ameliorate the consequences of WMD terrorism. Such a checklist could be used by citizens to hold their governments accountable for action or inaction.

Responsibility for preventing a WMD attack is not limited to the federal government; state and local governments have a critical role to play in helping to protect the nation. The next administration should work with a representative group of state and local governments to develop a simple checklist of steps for them to improve their ability to prevent such attacks. This checklist should be developed within the first six months of the next administration, and it should be made publicly available to enable citizens to hold their state and local governments accountable.

For instance, such a checklist should include adequate support for first responders and public health units. It might expand in metropolitan areas to funding for local police departments to ensure participation on local FBI-led Joint Terrorism Task Forces. These task forces serve, in effect, as the operational arm of domestic counterterrorism efforts, and state and local participation is vital to ensuring their success. Yet statements during Commission interviews and hearings made clear that the further local governments are removed in time from September 11, 2001, and the more distant they are from New York and Washington, D.C., the less priority they give to counterterrorism.

The Commission recognizes that many state and local governments are currently under enormous financial pressure. However, such challenges cannot be allowed to increase our nation's vulnerability to another attack. A checklist will give citizens a meaningful metric to evaluate their state and local governments' counterterrorism efforts, and though it may not ensure that minimum capabilities are maintained, it will help Americans understand the consequences of inadequate preparation.

ACTION: The federal government should seek to strengthen its ties with immigrant and second-generation populations, especially from the Middle East and Asia, to encourage greater engagement and investment by private U.S. citizens in improving the civil and cultural institutions of foreign partners.

The United States is a nation of immigrants, but the U.S. government is often slow to use this enormous asset when developing and implementing foreign outreach and assistance. A multitude of ethnic cultural and professional societies thrive within the United States and provide direct links to foreign countries. Given these resources, the government should engage immigrant groups and second- and third-generation citizens in supporting U.S. foreign assistance and institution-building efforts. These populations are often appreciative of the opportunities available to them in the United States and are supportive of U.S. government efforts to improve conditions in the countries of their or their family's origin. Yet as one senior official acknowledged to the Commission, "We simply haven't asked them to help."

Such informal assistance and engagement programs have the added benefit of directly supporting other recommendations made by the Commission, especially the recommendation to improve global ideological engagement. Immigrant or second- and third-generation populations are likely seen as more credible spokespeople than are representatives of the U.S. government.

> **ACTION:** As a priority of the next administration, the Secretary of Homeland Security should release a set of recommendations on which citizens can act to improve preparedness against potential WMD attacks. Such recommendations could range from following the Red Cross disaster preparedness guidelines to encouraging their workplaces and children's schools to prepare emergency plans.

There are simple steps that most individuals can take to mitigate the consequences of an attack—even a WMD attack. By demonstrating that they could reduce at a national level the potential damage and lasting effects caused by an attack, citizens might convince a terrorist organization that pursuing such an attack was not worth the effort and thus deter it.

The Department of Homeland Security, through its Ready.gov program, has sought to outline steps that Americans can take to prepare for potential attacks. This effort has received considerable criticism, however, both because communications during the initial rollout were poor and because the advice was too simplistic. The recommendations to purchase plastic sheeting and duct tape were roundly ridiculed, and in this critical first engagement with the public DHS lost credibility. Now, more than seven years since the 9/11 attacks, the public has also grown complacent.

The next administration has a chance to reengage the public in establishing a culture of preparedness. Within the first six months, the next Secretary of Homeland Security, building on the wide range of knowledge located in think tanks, state and local governments, universities, and other centers of expertise, should release a set of clear and specific actions that citizens can take to improve their preparedness for WMD attacks.

ACTION: Like the government, citizens should transform their involvement to meet the challenges of the 21st century. This includes holding political leaders accountable for the performance of the government in countering emerging threats.

Elsewhere in this report are recommendations for how Congress should reform to meet the challenges of this new security environment. While mandating at least two sweeping reforms of the executive branch, Congress has failed to substantively act on any recommendations to reform itself. No other branch of government has the authority to compel Congress to evolve to meet new challenges. Ultimately, the greatest stimulus of, and check on, the actions of Congress remains the American people.

○ ○ ○

On the day before the seventh anniversary of the infamous terrorist attacks on America's homeland, our Commission convened a public hearing in New York City. We marked the day, September 10, 2008, by hearing first from one whose family suffered a grievous loss in the attacks—Carie Lemack, a founder of Families of September 11. Then we heard from witnesses who shared insights that came from their work in government, the media, academia, and law enforcement. It was well into the day when Commissioner Raymond Kelly of the New York City Police Department testified. And in his presentation, he summed up with poignancy and urgency the challenge facing us all today—globally, nationally, locally, and in the one role we all share, as concerned citizens.

"Whether it's fixing gaping holes in regulation, securing loose nuclear materials abroad, or fully funding programs here at home that represent our last line of defense, we have absolutely no time to lose," Commissioner Kelly told the Commission. "Everything we know about al Qaeda tells us they will try to hit us again, possibly the next time with a weapon of mass destruction. We must do everything in our power to stop them before it's too late."

Appendices

Review of Implementation of the Baker-Cutler Report

Background

A Report Card on the Department of Energy's Nonproliferation Programs with Russia—perhaps better known as the Baker-Cutler report—was released in January 2001. It reflected the findings of a task force established by Secretary of Energy Bill Richardson and co-chaired by former Senate Majority Leader Howard Baker and former White House Counsel Lloyd Cutler that was tasked to "review and assess DOE's nonproliferation programs in Russia and make recommendations for their improvement." The Implementing Recommendations of the 9/11 Commission Act of 2007 directs this Commission to reassess and, where necessary, update the Baker-Cutler report and examine how effectively its recommendations have been implemented. This appendix addresses that legislative requirement. Part I examines Baker-Cutler recommendations and their implementation; part II reviews key programs designed to address nuclear security concerns in Russia, as administered by the Department of Energy through the National Nuclear Security Administration (NNSA).

Part I: Assessment

The Baker-Cutler report found that (1) the danger that nuclear weapons or weapons-usable material in Russia could be stolen and sold to terrorists or a hostile nation was the most urgent and unmet national security threat to the United States; (2) the budget levels for DOE's programs were inadequate and management of cooperative nonproliferation programs across the U.S. government too diffuse; and (3) the U.S. government needed to "develop an enhanced response proportionate to the threat."

Each of these findings were addressed by the Department of Energy. Recognizing the risks from undersecured nuclear materials in Russia, DOE accelerated efforts to better secure that material. The department also increased the budget for these and related efforts and, in recognition of the gravity of the threat, initiated a number of programs to complement nuclear materials security efforts.

The Baker-Cutler report specified six steps to be taken, calling on the United States to:

- **Formulate a strategic plan** to secure and/or neutralize in the next eight to ten years all nuclear weapons-usable material located in Russia and to prevent the outflow from Russia of scientific expertise that could be used for nuclear or other weapons of mass destruction;
- **Identify specific goals and measurable objectives** within the strategic plan and associated budgets for each program, as well as provide criteria for success and an exit strategy;
- **Accelerate the pace and increase funding** for specific programs in coordination with the strategic plan;
- Reach agreement with the Russian Federation at the highest level on **acceptable measures for transparency and access;**
- Improve coordination within the U.S. Government by establishing a **high-level leadership position in the White House;** and
- **Focus public and congressional attention** on this critical issue.

The report's principal recommendation—that a comprehensive strategic plan be formulated to address concerns over nuclear materials in Russia and stem the flow of expertise—was not implemented. However, the spirit of the Baker-Cutler recommendations—which aimed primarily at expanding and accelerating activity to secure nuclear materials in Russia—was clearly followed, accelerated significantly by the 2005 Bratislava Nuclear Security Initiative. One concern is that the program has not had access to all the sites in Russia where sensitive materials are stored, and it has proved difficult to get a comprehensive accounting from Russia of all its sites and facilities.

The United States also funded programs to reduce the prospect of scientist migration, the second principal substantive objective of the Baker-Cutler report. Yet the successes of these programs, though considerable, proved hard to quantify; and over time, changes were made as the security environment evolved. One of DOE's two programs (the Nuclear Cities Initiative) was eliminated. The other, the Initiatives for Proliferation Prevention (IPP), remains active but at lower funding levels than in the past.

The paragraphs below summarize the Commission's conclusions on the other steps called for by the Baker-Cutler report.

DOE has developed specific goals and objectives for its programs in Russia and the republics of the former Soviet Union, as well as metrics for gauging success and determining program budgets.

The funding and pace of activity in Russia have increased. Program-level strategic plans, though not specifically a product of the Baker-Cutler recommendation, are regularly developed, updated, and justified to senior management as part of the DOE planning process. But no government-wide strategic plan has been formulated to guide the department's activities in detail.

The record on the development of "exit strategies" is mixed. The fundamental mission in Russia—to secure nuclear materials there and transfer responsibility for maintaining nuclear security upgrades to Russia—has a clear end date mandated by Congress (2013), and it appears that this deadline will be met. Other programs, such as efforts to facilitate the shut down of Russia's plutonium producing reactors, are also on track to complete their work. However, programs such as DOE's efforts to engage nuclear scientists in civilian pursuits do not have clearly defined end points, although they have changed their approach to address threats as they are evolving. Nonetheless, the scientist engagement program would do well to further refine its definition of success and to ensure that its long-term objectives are commensurate with threat projections.

No White House–level coordination position has yet been established (as discussed in more detail in the body of this report). A senior advisor on WMD proliferation and terrorism could help augment and elevate public awareness of what the government is doing in this area. Currently, information is disseminated through the speeches, testimony, and public outreach efforts of DOE.

Programs to address plutonium in Russia—by facilitating the shutdown of reactors still producing it and by disposing of 34 metric tons of the material—are now on track. A significant amount of Russia's excess highly enriched uranium (HEU) is being eliminated, consistent with the Baker-Cutler objectives. At the same time, efforts are just now getting under way to undertake feasibility studies on converting Russian civilian research reactors from HEU to low-enriched uranium (LEU). The United States must urge Russia to accelerate this conversion and to work with the United States on a plan to make additional HEU available for blend-down (processing into a less-enriched form).

As a means to reduce U.S. costs, the Baker-Cutler report encouraged the U.S. government to press other nations to contribute to threat reduction programs in Russia. Shortly after the report was released, the G-8 Global Partnership, which committed G-8 and European Union states to contributing $20 billion over 10 years for threat reduction programs in Russia, was established. Half of this amount would come from the United States, and DOE programs are counted toward the U.S. share. The goal is close to being met. Among the principal contributors are Canada, Japan, other G-8 nations, and the European Union. In addition, the National Nuclear Security Administration has received more than $45 million in international contributions and pledges from seven countries. DOE/NNSA also has several cost-sharing partnerships in place that involve both monetary and in-kind contributions (equipment and training) from more than 20 countries.

Sustainability is a concern, however. Russia has not fully committed to increase resources for nuclear security upgrades as U.S. efforts come to completion, or taken steps to ensure that an adequate security culture will be in place in Russia after U.S. programs have ended. Russia's budgets to implement and sustain physical protection and security upgrades at both the site and national levels are unknown. Because Russia has not created a comprehensive baseline inventory, there are no reliable and comprehensive national accounting systems to monitor fissile material in Russia. Russia and NNSA are working together to build a federal database to track its proliferation-attractive nuclear material.

Overall, substantial progress has been made since 2001 in meeting the essential objectives in Russia articulated in the Baker-Cuter report. At the same time, there is ample opportunity for further progress. Securing Russian warheads and material must remain a priority. Without a solid and transparent commitment by Russia to maintain the level of security that has been implemented, the existing achievements are imperiled. It is important that the United States and Russia strengthen partnerships to secure and eliminate dangerous nuclear material, convert Russia's civil nuclear reactors from the use of HEU to LEU, and negotiate a transparency regime to support plutonium disposition (discussed below). In addition, securing Russia's borders and engaging scientists at targeted facilities in Russia in civilian pursuits should remain priority objectives. As the Baker-Cutler report emphasized, these efforts must be coordinated within the U.S. government to ensure maximum efficiency and effectiveness as the programs adapt to new challenges and as the United States and Russia shift from having a donor-recipient relationship to being partners.

Next Steps—"Updating" Baker-Cutler

Looked at narrowly—in terms only of U.S. nuclear security programs in Russia—the Baker-Cutler report has no need to be "updated." What is more important, as discussed in the section of our report titled "Nuclear Proliferation and Terrorism," is that, in effect, a new Baker-Cutler be undertaken in the form of a broad strategic review of cooperative nuclear security programs and nuclear security challenges worldwide, which include remaining work in Russia.

Appendices

As discussed in the text of this report, the Commission recommends that the next President conduct a bottom-up review of all threat reduction programs in the former Soviet Union (FSU) and throughout the world, to ensure that they are being implemented as effectively as possible, and that a strategy for addressing potential gaps in coverage be articulated. This assessment should identify programs that play a critical role worldwide and could be expanded; in addition, it should identify programs that may have achieved their objectives or outlived their usefulness and could therefore be reduced, reoriented, or eliminated. In weighing the possible expansion of programs to other nuclear weapons states, this review needs to evaluate the openness of such states to U.S. or international assistance. Finally, the review needs to assess what Russia may be willing to do in cooperation with the United States, particularly with respect to cost sharing, given its new, more active role in international affairs and the improvements in its economic status in the years since the Baker-Cutler report was produced.

Part II: Review and Assessment of Relevant Programs

Key programs evaluated by the Baker-Cutler commission included

- The Material Protection, Control, and Accounting (MPC&A) Program, which secures nuclear weapons and materials in Russia.
- The Highly Enriched Uranium (HEU) Purchase Agreement and Transparency Implementation Program, which is blending down 500 metric tons of HEU from Russia's weapons programs into fuel for use in the United States.
- The Russian Plutonium Disposition Program, which commits the United States and Russia to each eliminate 34 metric tons of plutonium declared in excess of defense requirements.
- The Second Line of Defense (SLD) program, which combats illicit trafficking of nuclear material and related equipment across Russia's borders.
- The Initiatives for Proliferation Prevention (IPP) Program and the Nuclear Cities Initiative (NCI), which implemented DOE's scientist engagement efforts (the programs were brought under common management in 2002; NCI projects in Russia's closed nuclear cities ended in 2005, and the program was not renewed).

Appendices

Material Protection, Control, and Accounting

The Baker-Cutler report noted that only a modest fraction of weapons-usable material had received comprehensive security upgrades, that disputes over access and transparency were undermining the broader context of cooperation, that no program was in place to sustain the work already done, and that a comprehensive testing and assessment program still awaited implementation.

Since the publication of the report, the MPC&A program, in close coordination with the Department of Defense, has accelerated U.S. cooperation with Russia on nuclear security. In February 2005, the United States and Russia signed the Bratislava Nuclear Security Initiative, which for the first time included a comprehensive plan for cooperation on security upgrades of Russian nuclear facilities at Federal Atomic Energy Agency (Rosatom) and Ministry of Defense sites. The MPC&A program is on track to complete these upgrades by the end of 2008.

Including sites added after the Bratislava Initiative was signed, the total scope of the MPC&A program now comprises 73 Russian nuclear warhead sites (65 upgraded by the end of fiscal year 2008) and 224 buildings containing nuclear material in Russia and other former Soviet countries (181 complete as of the end of FY 2008). While the precise number of sites containing nuclear material is not clear, these are believed to include the vast majority of overall sites. In the National Defense Authorization Act of 2003, Congress mandated that all responsibility for nuclear security work in Russia be transferred over to the Russian Federation by January 1, 2013. The MPC&A program expects to complete all security upgrades in Russia in 2012.

Consistent with the Baker-Cutler recommendations, MPC&A has made considerable progress in consolidating nuclear materials in fewer facilities. For example, the MPC&A program has eliminated special nuclear material (SNM) from 25 buildings at civilian-sector sites, including the removal of all highly enriched uranium from one civilian-sector site entirely. However, many Russian nuclear sites are apparently reluctant to give up nuclear material, either because they plan to restart dormant research and operations activity or because they wish to retain the prestige and worker benefits associated with a nuclear mission.

In 2007 the MPC&A program developed a Joint Sustainability Plan, signed by U.S. and Russian government officials, which requires Rosatom to sustain U.S.-provided physical protection upgrades installed over the past 14 years. The plan contains seven Sustainability Principles that outline at both the industry and site level the fundamental elements of sustainability—covering human resources, finances, and maintenance. NNSA and Rosatom are now developing a Joint Transition Plan, which will set forth estimated dates for completing the transfer of sustainability activities to Russian control. This plan will identify sustainability requirements for each site and establish timelines for the transfer of financial responsibility; NNSA continues to seek, but has not received, commitments from Rosatom to increase funding for site- and national-level MPC&A activities as part of the transition process.

Highly Enriched Uranium Transparency

NNSA expects to complete the blending down of 500 metric tons of Russia's HEU by 2013. However, Russia has shown little interest in continuing the process beyond that amount, in part because it believes that it may be able to get a better price for its downblended HEU from other countries. Legislation recently proposed by Senator Pete Domenici would improve Russia's access to the U.S. market, on the condition that Moscow blend down additional HEU beyond the 500 metric tons already agreed. The Commission believes that this is a sensible approach.

Russian Plutonium Disposition

The September 2000 Plutonium Management and Disposition Agreement (PMDA) committed the United States and Russia to each dispose of 34 metric tons of plutonium, but a number of obstacles slowed their progress. These included a disagreement over the path for disposing of the material, the liability of contractors working in the Russian Federation, financing, and the lack of a monitoring regime to provide confidence that the program would not lead to proliferation.

Over time, most of these issues were resolved; in November 2007, the United States and Russia agreed on a plan for Russia to dispose of the 34 metric tons of its plutonium as mixed oxide (MOX) fuel in Russia's fast reactors—the BN-600 and the BN-800, which is currently under construction. Russia has also pledged to bear most of the cost and could begin disposing of its plutonium by 2012. Under this plan, the U.S. contribution is capped at $400 million. Both the United States and Russia plan to complete disposition of all 68 metric tons of plutonium between 2035 and 2040. This schedule, subject to congressional funding, takes into account both the time needed to construct facilities in Russia and the United States and the time needed to actually dispose of the material.

One unresolved issue concerns the establishment of a monitoring and inspection regime. For years efforts have been made to negotiate such a regime, but Russian concerns over transparency and access have prevented an agreement from being reached.

Second Line of Defense

The Baker-Cutler report called for an increase in funding for the Second Line of Defense (SLD) program because, in the task force's judgment, the program was moving forward too slowly. In FY 2000, the program's budget was $6 million; by FY 2008, it was $267 million. In response to heightened concerns after 9/11, SLD work in the FSU countries has steadily and consistently expanded to other countries. SLD's Core Program installs radiation detection equipment at borders, airports, and strategic feeder ports, primarily in Russia and the former Soviet republics.

In 2006, the program reached an agreement with the Federal Customs Service of Russia to equip all 350 Russian border crossings with radiation detection equipment by the end of 2011. A total of 117 sites in Russia have been equipped to date, and costs for this effort are shared by NNSA and the Russian Customs Service. The Core Program has identified a total of 450 sites where detection equipment will be installed. The Megaports Initiative, launched in 2003, works with countries to equip seaports with radiation detection equipment. The program is operational in ports in 19 countries. Program officials have identified 75 ports altogether for potential cooperation.

Initiatives for Proliferation Prevention and Nuclear Cities Initiative

The Baker-Cutler report noted that the IPP suffered from years of inconsistent funding from Congress, and that metrics, such as the number of actual weapons scientists engaged in commercial jobs, were difficult to document. The report emphasized that careful attention should be given to defining criteria for success and developing an exit strategy for the program.

In 2005, DOE established the Global Initiatives for Proliferation Prevention (GIPP): it combined the missions of the IPP and the NCI, which worked with former scientists in Russia's closed nuclear cities, and expanded the scientist engagement mission beyond Russia and the former Soviet Union. GIPP has engaged thousands of former weapons scientists, engineers, and technicians at more than 180 facilities in the former Soviet Union, as well as hundreds of former weapons specialists in Libya and Iraq.

GIPP coordinates closely with the Department of State's Global Threat Reduction (GTR) program, which also works with former FSU weapons scientists and has expanded to include facilities in Iraq and Libya. As GIPP's original mission has evolved, it has reduced the scope of its work in the FSU to focus on institutes deemed potentially vulnerable to targeted recruitment. However, the program still has not developed a formal exit strategy.

Relevant Programs Initiated After the Baker-Cutler Report

Additional programs undertaken by DOE/NNSA consistent with Baker-Cutler objectives include the Elimination of Weapons Grade Plutonium Production (EWGPP) program, which is replacing Russia's last three plutonium-producing reactors with fossil fuel plants. Two of these reactors have already been shut down, and the third is scheduled to close no later than December 2010.

The Baker-Cutler report called for the return of HEU from Soviet-built research reactors to Russia for downblending and disposition. This is being accomplished through NNSA's Global Threat Reduction Initiative (GTRI), which is working to convert U.S.- and Russian-built HEU-fueled research reactors around the world to less-proliferation-sensitive LEU and to repatriate the HEU to its country of origin. To date, GTRI has helped return 764 kilograms of Russian-origin HEU from reactors for blending down. This total includes 21 HEU shipments from Soviet-built research reactors in Serbia, Romania, Bulgaria, Libya, Uzbekistan, the Czech Republic, Latvia, Poland, Germany, Hungary, and Vietnam. GTRI reports that it plans to remove or dispose of about 2,245 kilograms of Russian-origin HEU from civilian sites by 2015.

International Nonproliferation/Counterproliferation Treaties, Regimes, and Initiatives

Treaties in Force

Treaty on the Nonproliferation of Nuclear Weapons (NPT)

The NPT is designed to prevent the spread of nuclear weapons and weapons technology, promote cooperation in the peaceful uses of nuclear energy, and further the goal of achieving complete nuclear and general disarmament. It entered into force on March 5, 1970, and has 188 members. Only India, Israel, North Korea, and Pakistan are not members of the NPT.

The NPT establishes a safeguards system, which includes inspections of civilian nuclear facilities, to monitor compliance with the treaty. This safeguards system is administered by the International Atomic Energy Agency (IAEA). In 1997, the IAEA adopted an Additional Protocol that, when ratified by individual NPT members, gives the agency expanded safeguards authority and greater access to verify nuclear declarations.

Convention on the Prohibition of the Development, Production and Stockpiling of Bacteriological and Toxin Weapons (BWC)

The Biological and Toxin Weapons Convention (BWC) bans the development, production, acquisition, and retention of biological agents and toxins, weapons, and specialized means of delivery. It entered into force on March 26, 1975. There are currently 162 state parties to the BWC. Notable non-parties include North Korea, Syria, Egypt, and Israel.

Convention on the Physical Protection of Nuclear Material (CPPNM)

The CPPNM entered into force on February 7, 1987. It has 137 state parties. The convention is the only international legally binding agreement on the physical protection of nuclear material. An amendment to the convention negotiated in 2005 will strengthen it by requiring state parties to protect nuclear facilities and material in peaceful domestic use and storage as well as during transport. The amendment will enter into force following its ratification by two-thirds of the state parties to the convention.

Appendices

Strategic Arms Reduction Treaty (START)

START was signed by the United States and the Soviet Union in July 1991. It limits long-range nuclear forces—land-based intercontinental ballistic missiles (ICBMs), submarine-launched ballistic missiles (SLBMs), and heavy bombers—and contains complex verification provisions. In May 1992, Belarus, Kazakhstan, Russia, Ukraine, and the United States signed a protocol naming all five parties to the treaty. START entered into force in December 31, 1994. It will expire on December 31, 2009, unless the parties agree to extend it.

Strategic Offensive Reductions Treaty ("Moscow Treaty")

The Moscow Treaty was signed on May 24, 2002, and entered into force on June 1, 2003. The treaty requires the United States and Russia to reduce their strategic nuclear warheads to between 1,700 and 2,200 by December 31, 2012, at which time the treaty expires.

Treaties Negotiated but Not in Force

Comprehensive Nuclear Test Ban Treaty (CTBT)

The CTBT bans any nuclear weapon test explosion or any other nuclear explosion. The CTBT has not entered into force. The provisions of the treaty require the 44 states with nuclear reactors to ratify the treaty before it enters into force. In October 1999, the U.S. Senate failed to give its consent to ratification of the treaty. Nevertheless, the United States is observing a unilateral moratorium on nuclear tests.

Proposed Treaties

Fissile Material Cut-Off Treaty (FMCT)

A proposal that the international community negotiate a ban on the production of fissile material (plutonium and enriched uranium) that could be used in nuclear weapons is on the long-term negotiating agenda at the United Nations Conference on Disarmament in Geneva. Negotiations have been largely stalled since 1993.

Nonproliferation Regimes

Zangger Committee

In 1971, a group of seven NPT nuclear supplier nations formed the Nuclear Exporters Committee, known as the Zangger Committee, to assist in restricting nuclear trade as called for in Article III of the NPT. In 1974, the Zangger Committee compiled a list of nuclear export items that could be potentially useful for military applications and agreed that the transfer of items on the list would trigger a requirement for IAEA safeguards to ensure that the items were not used to make nuclear explosives.

Nuclear Suppliers Group (NSG)

In 1975, the major nuclear suppliers formed the London Club, which is now known as the Nuclear Suppliers Group (NSG). The NSG is an informal group of 45 nuclear supplier countries that seeks to halt proliferation of nuclear weapons through the implementation of guidelines for nuclear material and technology exports.

Executive Agreements

HEU Purchase Agreement

Under the United States–Russian Highly Enriched Uranium (HEU) Purchase Agreement, signed in 1993, 500 tons of HEU from dismantled Russian nuclear weapons is to be blended down to proliferation-resistant low-enriched uranium (LEU) by 2013. The United States Enrichment Corporation, a private corporation serving as executive agent for the HEU Purchase Agreement, purchases this LEU and resells it to U.S. companies that use it as commercial nuclear reactor fuel.

Plutonium Management and Disposition Agreement (PMDA)

Under the PMDA, signed in September 2000, the United States and Russia each agreed to dispose of 34 metric tons of weapons-grade plutonium. A series of disagreements were settled in a follow-on agreement in November 2007, with an overall understanding to complete the disposition of 68 metric tons total of plutonium between 2035 and 2040.

Nonproliferation/Counterproliferation Initiatives

Proliferation Security Initiative (PSI)

The PSI was launched in 2003 to increase international cooperation in interdicting shipments of weapons of mass destruction (WMD), their delivery systems, and related materials. As of October 2008, 92 nations have formally committed to PSI participation as partner states.

Appendices

Global Initiative to Combat Nuclear Terrorism (GICNT)

The GICNT was launched by the United States and Russia on July 15, 2006, to expand and accelerate the development of their partnership capacity to combat the global threat of nuclear terrorism. The GICNT is open to other partner nations, which currently number 75.

Bratislava Nuclear Security Initiative

President Vladimir Putin and President George W. Bush agreed to this initiative on nuclear security cooperation at a February 2005 summit in Bratislava, the Republic of Slovakia. The Bratislava Nuclear Security Initiative is focused on five key areas: emergency response cooperation, sharing best practices to promote nuclear security, enhancing nuclear security cultures in both countries, research reactor conversion and fuel return, and promoting the implementation of UNSCR 1540. A senior U.S.-Russia group chaired by the U.S. Secretary of Energy and the Director of the Federal Atomic Energy Agency (Rosatom) oversees this work and provides progress reports to the Presidents every six months.

United Nations Security Council Resolution 1540

UNSCR 1540 is a 2004 resolution that establishes binding obligations on all UN member states to take and enforce measures against WMD proliferation, such as developing the laws and regulations they need to criminalize proliferation, improving physical protection and safeguards at nuclear facilities, strengthening export controls, and developing a robust security culture focused on reducing the risk of theft or diversion of nuclear materials or technology.

Acronyms and Abbreviations

AMI	American Media International
BSL	Biosafety Level
BW	Biological Weapons
BWC	Biological Weapons Convention
CDC	Centers for Disease Control and Prevention
CIA	Central Intelligence Agency
CP	counterproliferation
CPPNM	Convention for the Physical Protection of Nuclear Material
CSI	Container Security Initiative
CT	counterterrorism
CTBT	Comprehensive Test Ban Treaty
CTR	cooperative threat reduction
DHS	Department of Homeland Security
DNI	Director of National Intelligence
DOE	Department of Energy
EU	European Union
EWGPP	Elimination of Weapons Grade Plutonium Production
FATA	Federally Administered Tribal Areas
FBI	Federal Bureau of Investigation
FMCT	Fissile Material Cut-Off Treaty
FSU	former Soviet Union
G-8	Group of Eight
GAO	Government Accountability Office
GICNT	Global Initiative to Combat Nuclear Terrorism
GIPP	Global Initiatives for Proliferation Prevention
GSPC	Salafist Group for Preaching and Combat (Groupe Salafiste pour la Prédication et le Combat)
GTRI	Global Threat Reduction Initiative
HEU	highly enriched uranium
HHS	Department of Health and Human Services
HSC	Homeland Security Council
IAEA	International Atomic Energy Agency
ICBM	Intercontinental Ballistic Missile

IHR	International Health Regulations
INFCIRC	Information Circular
IPP	Initiatives for Proliferation Prevention
LEU	low-enriched uranium
MOX	mixed oxide
MPC&A	Material Protection, Control and Accounting
NCI	Nuclear Cities Initiative
NCPC	National Counterproliferation Center
NCTC	National Counterterrorism Center
NNSA	National Nuclear Security Administration
NPT	Nonproliferation Treaty
NSC	National Security Council
NWFP	North-West Frontier Province
ODNI	Office of the Director of National Intelligence
OIE	World Organization for Animal Health (formerly known as the Office international des épizooties)
PCC	Policy Coordinating Committee
PMDA	Plutonium Management and Disposition Agreement
PSI	Proliferation Security Initiative
Rosatom	[Russian] Federal Atomic Energy Agency
SARS	severe acute respiratory syndrome
SLBM	submarine-launched ballistic missile
SLD	Second Line of Defense
SNM	special nuclear material
START	Strategic Arms Reduction Treaty
UNSCR	United Nations Security Council Resolution
USAID	U.S. Agency for International Development
USDA	United States Department of Agriculture
WHO	World Health Organization
WMD	Weapons of Mass Destruction

Commissioner Biographies

Senator Bob Graham, Commission Chairman, is a former two–term governor of Florida and served for 18 years in the United States Senate. This is combined with 12 years in the Florida legislature for a total of 38 years of public service. In the Senate, he served on the Select Committee on Intelligence—including eighteen months as chairman in 2001–2002. During this time, he served as co-chairman of the joint House-Senate inquiry of the events surrounding the September 11th attacks. Following the release of the Joint Inquiry's final report in July 2003, Senator Graham steadfastly advocated reform of the intelligence community and sponsored legislation to bring about needed changes. Based on these experiences, he authored *Intelligence Matters*.

After retiring from the Senate in 2004, Senator Graham served for a year as a senior fellow at the Harvard Kennedy School of Government. His primary focus was on civic education and intelligence. While there, he commenced research and writing a book, to be published early 2009, entitled *America, The Owner's Manual*. He has established a Center for Public Service at the University of Florida and the University of Miami, which primarily focuses on participatory citizenship, homeland security and the Americas. He received his bachelors degree from the University of Florida and his law degree from Harvard Law School.

Senator Jim Talent, Commission Vice-Chairman, was elected at the age of 28 to the Missouri House of Representatives, where he served for eight years, beginning in 1984. At the age of 32, Senator Talent was unanimously chosen by his colleagues to be the Minority Leader, the highest-ranking Republican leadership position in the Missouri House. He served in that capacity until 1992, when he was elected to Congress to represent Missouri's Second District; he served in the House until 2001.

While in the House, Senator Talent served for eight years on the House Armed Services Committee. In 2002, Missourians elected Talent to the United States Senate, where he served until 2007. During that time, he served as the Chairman of the Armed Services Seapower Subcommittee.

Currently, Senator Talent serves as a Distinguished Fellow at the Washington, D.C.–based Heritage Foundation, where he specializes in military readiness issues and welfare reform. Senator Talent received his bachelor's degree from Washington University in St. Louis, where he received the Arnold J. Lien Prize as the most outstanding undergraduate in political science. He graduated Order of the Coif from the University of Chicago Law School in 1981 and clerked for Judge Richard Posner of the United States Court of Appeals from 1982 through 1983.

Appendices

Graham Allison is Douglas Dillon Professor of Government and Director of the Belfer Center for Science and International Affairs at Harvard's John F. Kennedy School of Government. Dr. Allison's most recent book, *Nuclear Terrorism: The Ultimate Preventable Catastrophe,* is now in its third printing and was selected by the *New York Times* as one of the "100 most notable books of 2004."

From 1977 to 1989, Dr. Allison served as Dean of the Kennedy School. Under his leadership, a small, undefined program grew twentyfold to become a major professional school of public policy and government.

From 1985 to 1987, Dr. Allison served as Special Advisor to the Secretary of Defense; from 1993 to 1994, as Assistant Secretary of Defense for Policy and Plans. He has the sole distinction of having twice been awarded the Defense Department's highest civilian award, the Distinguished Public Service Medal, first by Secretary Casper Weinberger and then by Secretary William Perry.

Dr. Allison has authored or co-authored 20 books and hundreds of articles. He has been a member of the Secretary of Defense's Defense Policy Board for Secretaries Weinberger, Carlucci, Cheney, Aspin, Perry, and Cohen. He was a founding member of the Trilateral Commission, was a Director of the Council on Foreign Relations, and has been a member of many public committees and commissions. He was educated at Davidson College, and he earned a B.A. in history at Harvard College; B.A. and M.A. degrees in philosophy, politics, and economics at Oxford University; and his Ph.D. at Harvard University.

Robin Cleveland currently serves as a Principal with Olivet Consulting LLC. Previously, she has served as the Counselor to the President of the World Bank, Associate Director at the White House Office of Management and Budget, and in a variety of key positions with Senator Mitch McConnell on the Senate Intelligence Committee, Senate Foreign Relations Committee, and Senate Appropriations Committee.

Ms. Cleveland co-led efforts to develop two presidential initiatives, the Millennium Challenge Corporation and the President's Emergency Plan for AIDS Relief, undertakings that reflect her experience linking policy, performance, and resource management. Ms. Cleveland graduated from Wesleyan University with honors.

Stephen G. Rademaker became Senior Counsel to BGR Holding LLC in January 2007. He continues to serve as the U.S. representative on the UN Secretary General's Advisory Board on Disarmament Matters, a position he has held since 2003.

Mr. Rademaker came to BGR Holding from the staff of Senate Majority Leader Bill Frist, where he served as Policy Director for National Security Affairs and Senior Counsel.

In 2002, Mr. Rademaker was confirmed by the Senate as an Assistant Secretary of State, and from then until 2006 he headed at various times three bureaus of the Department of State, including the Bureau of Arms Control and the Bureau of International Security and Nonproliferation. He directed nonproliferation policy toward Iran and North Korea, as well as the Proliferation Security Initiative.

Immediately prior to joining the Department of State, Rademaker was Chief Counsel to the Select Committee on Homeland Security of the U.S. House of Representatives, where he was responsible for drafting the legislation that created the Department of Homeland Security.

Mr. Rademaker has also held positions on the staff of the Committee on International Relations of the House of Representatives, including Deputy Staff Director and Chief Counsel.

From 1992 to 1993, Mr. Rademaker served as General Counsel of the Peace Corps. He returned briefly to the agency in 2000–2001 as the Bush-Cheney transition's Director of Transition for the Peace Corps.

Mr. Rademaker received three degrees from the University of Virginia: a B.A. with Highest Distinction in 1981, a J.D. in 1984, and an M.A. in foreign affairs in 1985. While at the University of Virginia he was made a member of Phi Beta Kappa and the Order of the Coif.

Congressman Timothy J. Roemer served in the U.S. House from 1991 to 2003. After the attacks of September 11, Mr. Roemer used his position on the House Permanent Select Committee on Intelligence to support the work of a joint congressional inquiry into the attacks. Mr. Roemer also was the key sponsor of legislation to establish the National Commission on Terrorist Attacks Upon the United States, better known as the 9/11 Commission. He went on to serve as a member of the 9/11 Commission.

Since leaving Congress in 2003, Mr. Roemer has continued to work on developing ways to strengthen national security as President of the Center for National Policy and as a Distinguished Scholar at the Mercatus Center at George Mason University.

Prior to his elected service, Mr. Roemer served on the staffs of Representative John Brademas of Indiana (1978–1979) and Senator Dennis DeConcini of Arizona (1985–1989).

He holds a Ph.D. in American government from the University of Notre Dame. Mr. Roemer also earned his M.A. from Notre Dame and received his B.A. from the University of California, San Diego.

Wendy R. Sherman is a Principal of The Albright Group LLC, a global strategy firm, and of Albright Capital Management LLC, an investment advisory firm focused on emerging markets.

During the Clinton administration, Ambassador Sherman served as Counselor and chief troubleshooter for the State Department, as well as Special Advisor to President Clinton and Policy Coordinator on North Korea.

She serves on the Board of Directors of Oxfam America and the Board of Advisors for the Center for a New American Security, and is a member of the Council on Foreign Relations and the Aspen Strategy Group. She is also a member of the U.S.-India Strategic Dialogue and a regular participant in the Australian American Leadership Dialogue. Ambassador Sherman attended Smith College, and she earned a B.A. *cum laude* from Boston University and a master's in social work, Phi Kappa Phi, from the University of Maryland.

Henry D. Sokolski is the Executive Director of the Nonproliferation Policy Education Center. From 1989 to 1993, Sokolski served as Deputy for Nonproliferation Policy in the Office of the Secretary of Defense and received the Secretary of Defense's Medal for Outstanding Public Service. Prior to that appointment, Mr. Sokolski worked in the Secretary's Office of Net Assessment on proliferation issues.

From 1984 to 1988, Mr. Sokolski served as Senior Military Legislative Aide to Senator Dan Quayle; from 1982 through 1983, he served as Special Assistant on Nuclear Energy Matters to Senator Gordon Humphrey.

Mr. Sokolski also served as a consultant on proliferation issues to the intelligence community's National Intelligence Council. After his work in the Pentagon, Mr. Sokolski received a congressional appointment to the Deutch Proliferation Commission, which completed its work in 1999. He also served as a member of the Central Intelligence Agency's Senior Advisory Panel from 1995 to 1996.

Mr. Sokolski has authored and edited numerous works on proliferation-related issues, including *Best of Intentions: America's Campaign Against Strategic Weapons Proliferation*. He attended the University of Southern California and Pomona College, received his graduate education at the University of Chicago, and currently teaches nuclear proliferation issues at the Institute of World Politics in Washington, D.C.

Rich Verma is a partner at the law firm of Steptoe & Johnson LLP, where he practices international law and is also a member of the firm's government affairs practice. Most recently, Mr. Verma served as Senior National Security Advisor to the Senate Majority Leader, a position he held for several years. Mr. Verma also worked as Senior Counsel and Policy Director for the Senate Whip and served on the staff of Congressman John P. Murtha.

Mr. Verma is a veteran of the U.S. Air Force and a former country director for the National Democratic Institute for International Affairs. He holds degrees from the Georgetown University Law Center, American University's Washington College of Law, and Lehigh University. He is a member of the Council on Foreign Relations, was formerly an International Affairs Fellow of the Council, and has served on the National Academy of Sciences Panel on Critical Infrastructure Protection and the Law.

Commission Staff

Evelyn N. Farkas, *Executive Director*
Eric K. Fanning, *Deputy Director*
Raj De, *General Counsel*

Amir M. Abdmishani
Professional Staff Member
Georgia A. Adams
Professional Staff Member
Amy A. Berg
Staff Assistant
Jennifer C. Boone
Professional Staff Member
Sylvia Boone
Administrative Officer
Robert DiNardo
Professional Staff Member
Andrew B. Duberstein
Intern
Alice Falk
Editor Copyeditor
Thomas W. Graham
Professional Staff Member
Stephen G. Heil
Professional Staff Member
Joseph Helman
Director for Intelligence
Adam J. Jones
Professional Staff Writer
Abraham C. Kanter
Staff Assistant
Sam E. Kessler
Special Assistant to the Executive Director
George W. Look
Director for Nonproliferation/Counterproliferation

Erin R. Mahan
Professional Staff Member
Maurice A. Mallin
Professional Staff Member
David E. McCracken
Professional Staff Member
Jamison D. Pirko
Staff Assistant
Neal A. Pollard
Director for Counterterrorism
Don A. Puglisi
Professional Staff Member
William R. Reed
Professional Staff Member
Constance T. Rybka
Chief of Security
Martin Schram
Consultant
Wade R. Sharp
Security Officer
Jonathan B. Tucker
Professional Staff Member
Jenee B. Tyler
Intern
Adam K. VanDervort
Professional Staff Member
Kenneth D. Ward
Professional Staff Member